Dynamic Models of
Advertising Competition

International Series in
Quantitative Marketing

Editor:
Jehoshua Eliasberg
The Wharton School
University of Pennsylvania
Philadelphia, Pennsylvania, U.S.A.

Previously published books in the series:

Cooper, L. and Nakanishi, M.: MARKET SHARE
 ANALYSIS
Hanssens, D., Parsons, L., and Schultz, R.:
 MARKET RESPONSE MODELS:
 ECONOMETRIC AND TIME SERIES
 ANALYSIS

McCann, J., and Gallagher, J.: EXPERT
 SYSTEMS FOR SCANNER DATA
 ENVIRONMENTS

Dynamic Models of Advertising Competition

Open- and Closed-Loop Extensions

Gary M. Erickson
University of Washington

Kluwer Academic Publishers
Boston/Dordrecht/London

Distributors for North America:
Kluwer Academic Publishers
101 Philip Drive
Assinippi Park
Norwell, Massachusetts 02061 USA

Distributors for all other countries:
Kluwer Academic Publishers Group
Distribution Centre
Post Office Box 322
3300 AH Dordrecht, THE NETHERLANDS

Library of Congress Cataloging-in-Publication Data

Erickson, Gary M., 1945–
    Dynamic models of advertising competition: open- and closed-
loop extensions / Gary M. Erickson.
        p.   cm.—(International series in quantitative marketing)
    Includes bibliographical references and index.
    ISBN 0-7923-9146-2 (alk. paper)
    1. Advertising—Mathematical models.   2. Competition—
Mathematical models.   I. Title.   II. Series.
HF5821.E75   1991   91-2344
659.1'01'5118—dc20   CIP

Printed on acid-free paper.

Printed in the United States of America

Contents

Preface

For years, I have been impressed by how dynamic markets are. Marketing strategies are rarely successful without adjustments over time, and marketing managers need constantly to monitor, and anticipate when possible, important changes in the marketing environment, so that they can adapt their marketing strategies to changing market conditions. It strikes me as important that the dynamic elements of marketing be modeled and studied, and a significant part of my research activity has been dedicated to exploring the nature and implications of dynamic marketing strategies.

The marketing field has used various models and methodologies in the attempt to understand dynamic markets. I must thank my dissertation advisor, Dave Montgomery at Stanford, for originally turning my attention toward time-varying parameter models some 14 years ago. From that platform, I have proceeded to search for models that capture the essence of dynamic marketing, as well as for methodological tools, empirical as well as analytical, that allow insightful study of such models.

Much of the dynamism seen in markets can be attributed to competition, and efforts to understand the role of dynamic marketing competition strike me as being especially valuable and insightful. I was introduced to one model in particular, the Lanchester model, through a 1979 review by John Little. The Lanchester model continues to impress me as one that is elegantly simple while containing both the competitive and dynamic essence of marketing—and in particular advertising—situations. Other models as well, in particular the Vidale–Wolfe and new-product diffusion models, have been the subjects of many research efforts in marketing and management science and continue to have potential for insight regarding dynamic marketing competition.

The present monograph is an analytical exploration into the differences and similarities between two types of solution concepts, open-loop and closed-loop, that can be defined in models of advertising competition that are interpreted as differential games. I particularly wish to thank the series editor of the developing *International Series in Quantitative Marketing*, Josh Eliashberg, for providing both encouragement and advice regarding the monograph. Zachary Rolnik, Editor with Kluwer Academic Publishers, has also been extremely helpful and supportive. It helps immensely to have the support of people like Josh and Zachary, who have generously allowed me to pursue this investigation into dynamic advertising competition. Also, I must acknowledge the extremely helpful comments of two reviewers, which have helped improve the monograph greatly.

Finally, I would like to express my appreciation for the professional leave of absence, granted by the University of Washington for Autumn Quarter, 1989, which helped greatly in the completion of the monograph.

Gary M. Erickson
Seattle, Washington

Dynamic Models of
Advertising Competition

1 ADVERTISING AND COMPETITION

A critical aspect of the advertising budgeting process involves competitive issues—anticipated spending levels of major competitors, effects that competitive advertising may have on the firm's market share, sales, and profit, and the interactive nature of a competitor's advertising with a firm's own. Competition is ignored only at the firm's peril; empirical studies (e.g., Little 1979; also see the empirical survey below) have shown quite clearly that competitive advertising can have a direct, and negative, effect on a company's market share. Also, management practice appears to recognize the importance of competition; in a survey of leading U.S. advertisers, Lancaster and Stern (1983) reveal that, among various general characteristics describing the advertising budgeting process, "competitive effects" were considered by 52% of the sample (second only to "communication effects" at 55%).

Advertising competition is both dynamic and interactive. Also, in certain markets, advertising is the primary competitive marketing tool. A case in point is the beer industry, which has evolved into a market in which heavy advertising expenditures are necessary not only to succeed but also to survive. The current situation has two companies, Anheuser-Busch with 40% of the market and Miller with 21%, "threatening to run away with the beer business" (*Business Week* 1989). The two market leaders are also

1

the largest advertisers in the industry, a situation that began in the early 1970s, when Miller was acquired by Philip Morris Inc. Miller's aggressive expansion after the acquisition led to a dynamic interplay of advertising competition with Anheuser-Busch, which responded with major increases in advertising spending. Anheuser-Busch "declared all-out war on Miller" (*Business Week* 1982, p. 52). The result has been a dramatic increase in Anheuser-Busch's market share—an increase from 30% in 1981 (*Business Week* 1982) to 40% currently (*Business Week* 1989)—although only some-what at the expense of Miller, which has seen a slight decline in share from 22% in 1981 to 21% currently. The remainder of Anheuser-Busch's increase in market share has come from smaller brands with lower advertising outlays than either Anheuser-Busch or Miller.

Advertising has long been a popular topic for academic research, not only in marketing but in the management science literature as well (see Hanssens, Parsons, and Schultz 1990 for an extensive treatment of the research area involving market response to advertising as well as other marketing decision variables). A variety of empirical studies of aggregate response to advertising (for reviews, see Clarke 1976; Little 1979; Aaker and Carman 1982; Assmus, Farley, and Lehmann 1984) have added to our knowledge of the extent to which advertising spending affects a product's sales, the basis for systematic variation in advertising effects, the shape of the response relationship between sales and advertising, and the dynamics of the advertising-sales relationship. In addition, theoretical studies of optimal advertising policies (see Sethi 1977; Feichtinger, Hartl, and Sethi 1989; Hahn and Hyun 1990) have provided insights into the optimal determination of dynamic advertising budgets. Much of the research to date, however, has focused only on single products, as if such products were operating in monopolistic markets, and has tended to suppress important aspects of the marketing environment, in particular the competition that takes place among products.

This is not to say that competitive aspects have been ignored in studies of advertising expenditures. A number of studies, both empirical and analytical, have attempted to probe the nature of advertising competition. We defer to the next chapter a survey and discussion of analytical ap-proaches. In the present chapter, we review the insights that have been gained through empirical analysis of competitive advertising.

Empirical Research

Telser (1962) provides a seminal empirical study with an examination of the marginal effectiveness of advertising in a competitive setting, the cigarette industry. In the study, brand market shares are related to relative advertising (a brand's advertising relative to the total advertising of competing brands) as well as to lagged market share. Telser's study involves the analysis of multiple brands in the attempt to provide a clear picture of the competition among the various brands in the market. In contrast, various other studies (Bass and Parsons 1969; Sexton 1970; Schultz 1971; Prasad and Ring 1976; Wittink 1977) are concerned only with the advertising effects of a single brand, although competition is recognized in the form of the total advertising of the remaining brands. Still others (Cowling et al. 1975, Brown 1978) pool data across brands, and time periods, to estimate a single relationship. Weiss (1968, 1969) and Peles (1971a, b) pool across brands, but also include dummy vriables that are brand specific or indicative of some aspect that varies across brands. It is worth noting that the estimated coefficients of such dummy variables are often statistically significant, indicating the general importance of not constraining effects to be equal across competing brands.

The study of advertising effects across multiple brands, in which the market shares of the brands are related in a regression framework to either relative advertising or advertising shares, has involved a number of extensions (Samuels 1971; Beckwith 1972; Lambin 1972; Schnabel 1972; Clarke 1973, 1978; Houston and Weiss 1974; Picconi and Olson 1978). Generally, the models estimated have been linear in terms of the variables or logarithms of the variables. A critical problem with such models is that they are not "logically consistent" (McGuire et al. 1968); that is, the market shares of the brands are not constrained to sum to a value of one. Logical consistency requires constraints on linear model parameters that are likely to be unrealistic, if Schmalensee's study of the cigarette market is any indication (Schmalensee 1972); Schmalensee finds that the constraints that must hold are rejected on the basis of sample information. A better approach, perhaps, would be to estimate models that are by design logically consistent, such as the multiplicative competitive interaction (MCI) model (Nakanishi and Cooper 1974), which can be linearized in terms of logarithms along with period- and brand-specific dummy variables (Nakanishi and Cooper 1982). The study by Carpenter et al. (1988) provides an empirical application of the MCI model. Also see Cooper and Nakanishi (1988).

Telser's work and most subsequent studies involve a dynamic aspect in the sense that advertising effects are assumed to carry over across time periods. The carryover effects are operationalized by including a lagged-market-share term as an explanatory variable. Certain studies, on the other hand (Kuehn, McGuire, and Weiss 1966; Bass 1969a; Bemmaor

1984) assume only current period effects of advertising on market share. A different dynamic approach is to model and estimate *changes* in market share as being influenced by advertising, as in Horsky (1977), Kelton and Kelton (1982), and Nguyen (1987). This approach can be interpreted as an aggregated modeling of consumer brand-switching behavior (Schmalensee 1978). It also allows and encourages the estimation of such models as the *Lanchester* model, which attributes dynamic changes in market share to a brand's attracting share from competitors through its own advertising and losing share to competing brands due to their advertising. The Lanchester model has been recommended for its ability to capture both dynamic and competitive effects, in addition to having other desirable qualities (Little 1979).

An important empirical issue, in addition to measuring advertising's effects on market share or change in share, involves the advertising budgeting decision, i.e., how advertising levels are set by the competitors in a market. A firm is likely to consider competitive spending levels in determining its own advertising budget, whether by anticipating what competitors will spend or by reacting to competitive spending levels on a lagged basis. Various researchers have investigated this issue. For example, Lambin (1970a) detects a positive competitive reaction to an increase in the advertising spending for the product under study. Metwally (1975) also detects positive competitive advertising reactions for various selected firms. Curiously, Metwally considers the competitive reaction to occur in the same time period, and not on a lagged basis. Grabowski and Mueller (1971) estimate lagged reactions of various cigarette firms to each other, and generally find positive reactions. Hanssens (1980) offers a more general model, including multiple marketing variables and allowing intra-firm reaction, as well. Fitting the model to data from an air travel market, Hanssens finds limited advertising reactions. The smallest of the three airlines in the market appears to be the advertising leader, and the other two airlines appear to react to the small airline's advertising, on a four-quarter lagged basis and in the same direction.

Roberts and Samuelson (1988) investigate whether firms anticipate competitive advertising reactions when they set their advertising budgets. A system of equations is estimated that involves market shares, production cost, factor demand, and choice of advertising goodwill levels. In the advertising goodwill choice relationships, dynamic conjectural variations, i.e., anticipation of competitive advertising reactions, are allowed for. Roberts and Samuelson find that firms determine their advertising goodwill levels as if they expect *negative* competitive reactions, that is, as if they expect competitors to *reduce* their advertising in response to an increase in their own, a finding which would appear to conflict with the generally positive reactions estimated in other empirical research.

Various other research efforts interpret the advertising decision as part of a system of relationships, generally viewing a firm's advertising as being influenced by lagged competitive advertising, lagged own advertising, and the firm's sales or market share, either on a lagged or a contemporaneous basis. (In addition, other variables, e.g., price, may be included if the study is analyzing multiple marketing instruments.) If advertising is affected contemporaneously by sales or market share, simultaneous-equation estimation is required. In a study of three brands, Lambin (1970b) finds advertising levels to respond in a positive manner to lagged market share, as well as to lagged rival advertising. In a later study involving a number of Western European industries, Lambin (1976) finds a general pattern of positive advertising reactions, but is unable to detect a systematic relationship involving the influence of market share. Wildt (1974) finds limited reaction in terms of advertising, in that one of three competitors responds positively to one of its rival's advertising, and another competitor reacts in a positive way to its own lagged market share. In a simultaneous-equations estimation, Lambin, Naert, and Bultez (1975) find that a market leader's advertising levels respond positively both to lagged competitive advertising (competitive advertising is not included as an endogenous variable in the system, but in a single-equation regression is estimated to react positively to the leader's advertising) and to contemporaneous market share. In a study involving various industries, Metwally (1978) finds a general pattern of positive reaction to both contemporaneous market share and to lagged rival advertising. In another multi-industry analysis, however, Lancaster (1984) finds no such general pattern. The Lancaster study involves pooling of data across brands, however, which may have affected the results. Two additional studies (Cowling et al. 1975; Brown 1978) offer analysis of pooled data. In both studies, simultaneity between a firm's advertising and sales is assumed, but rival advertising is not included as a determinant of the firm's advertising. Interestingly, a *negative* effect of sales on advertising is estimated in both studies. Finally, Bass (1969a) aggregates cigarette brands into filter and monfilter types and analyzes a system of simultaneous equations involving sales and advertising of the two types of cigarettes. Bass finds a positive effect of filter sales on advertising of filter cigarettes, and a negative effect of nonfilter cigarette sales on nonfilter advertising.

To summarize the empirical literature on advertising competition, much in the way of results, even consistent results, has been generated, but little insight has been gained. We have a situation in which the empirical work has outpaced theoretical understanding. Studies of response to advertising report findings of positive competitive reaction in terms of advertising, which by implication leads to escalating advertising "wars." Such wars would have their natural limits, and can therefore be only temporary phenomena. Also unresolved is why, as Roberts and Samuelson (1988) find, firms anticipate negative competitive reactions in terms of advertising levels, when just the opposite is detected in other studies. Further, the results presuppose a leader–follower type of competitive arrangement, which can be a complicated and ill-defined situation, in that certain of the reaction models have that leaders can also be followers. Other important competitive models have not been studied empirically to any substantial degree, in particular the situation in which competitors make their advertising decisions *simultaneously* (in an information sense)—each competitor determines its advertising strategy, inferring the strategies of the other competitors but without actually observing their decisions (Eliashberg and Chatterjee 1985). A *differential game* formulation (Case 1979) can be used to treat simultaneous decisions in a dynamic setting, but empirical investigation of differential game models is at a very early stage; Chintagunta and Vilcassim (1989) provide an example of such an analysis.

The empirical literature is even less consistent regarding the effect that a brand's sales level or market share has on advertising expenditures for the brand. Both positive and negative effects have been detected. At any rate, little theoretical work, in the area of dynamic and competitive decision models, has been devoted the study of how marketing variables respond dynamically to variables such as market share. As will be seen in chapter 2, most work in this area has concentrated on what are termed *open-loop* solutions, which can vary only with time, and are not allowed to depend on the level of sales or market share beyond the beginning of the planning horizon. To allow competitive advertising levels to vary with changing sales or shares requires the study of *closed-loop* solutions, which can vary not only with time but with other important variables as well. These concepts will be developed more fully in subsequent chapters.

Plan of the Monograph

From this point, the primary emphasis will be on the analytical study of advertising competition. As we shall see, existing analytical research has made some contributions, but it is need of extension. Chapter 2 discusses game theory concepts that are useful in analyzing dynamic advertising rivalries, reviews the existing literature on analytical approaches to the problem, and introduces models and solution concepts to be used in later chapters. Chapters 3, 4, and 5 offer both open-loop and closed-loop (specifically, the *perfect equilibrium* concept of Case (1979)) analyses of three different competitive advertising scenarios. Open-loop and closed-loop advertising strategies are compared. Finally, chapter 6 discusses related issues and summarizes what is learned through the research efforts presented in the monograph.

2 ANALYTICAL MODELS AND STRATEGY CONCEPTS

As Eliashberg and Chatterjee (1985) indicate, the analytical study of competition requires that certain basic assumptions be made regarding the number of competitors to be studied, the nature of competitive interaction, and the information base of the competitors involved. Generally, studies to date have assumed a game theory framework, in which each of the various competitors involved is a decision-maker, although some (e.g., Horsky 1977) study only the decisions of a single competitor. A game theory framework offers a potentially rich setting for studying the interactive nature of competitive advertising. It has usually been assumed in previous research that the competitors make their advertising decisions simultaneously and with complete information. (Bensoussan, Bultez, and Naert (1978), on the other hand, view the situation as a sequential decision-making process, and adopt the perspective of the market leader that needs to anticipate the reactions of its competitors to its decisions.) That is, each competitor has full knowledge of the nature of the competitive interaction and the motivations and profit structures of the other competitors, so that each competitor can infer with certainty the strategies of its rivals. Also, it is generally assumed that the competitors cannot collude (although Wrather and Yu (1979) suggest that some cooperation may be involved, in

9

the situation in which advertising can be used to expand the market.) Assuming collusion is not possible, the *noncooperative* branch of game theory is appealed to, and *Nash equilibria* are sought to define the advertising strategies of the competitors. A Nash equilibrium is a list of strategies, one for each competitor, which has the property that no competitor would like unilaterally to change its strategy (Moorthy 1985); in a Nash equilibrium, each strategy is a competitor's best strategy, given the strategies of its rivals, where "best" is defined according to the competitor's objectives (e.g., to maximize profit). Finally, most studies to date have involved a duopoly, or exactly two competitors, although a triopoly (three competitors) appears occasionally (e.g., Teng and Thompson 1983), and recent efforts have been made to extend analysis to a general number of competitors (Dockner and Jørgensen 1990; Tang 1990). In most situations, it is difficult, if not impossible, to analyse the decisions of a general number of competitors. At the same time, it is important to study situations involving direct competition among a small number of firms, in which the marketing activities of the competing firms directly affect and are recognized by each other. Analyzing a duopoly, in particular, would seem to capture important basic elements of direct competition, certainly of the one-on-one variety. Also, a duopoly assumption may not be terribly limiting, in that many real-life marketing situations appear to mimic such a situation, especially when advertising is involved (e.g., Coke versus Pepsi, Budweiser versus Miller).

Early game theory applications of advertising competition (Friedman 1958; Mills 1961; Shakun 1965; Gupta and Krishnan 1967; Schmalensee 1976) emphasized *static* models. Alternatively, such competition can be viewed as a *dynamic* situation, in which advertising by the competitors can change across time. The latter, dynamic mode is preferable, in that it adds the important dimension of time and recognizes that competitive decisions do not necessarily remain fixed. Competitive markets are inherently dynamic, and models that recognize this basic reality offer the potential for great insight into competitive advertising strategies. A dynamic competitive situation can be analyzed in terms of either *discrete* or *continuous* time. See Shakun (1966) and Zufryden (1975) as examples of discrete-time models. Continuous-time models are clearly an abstraction of reality, but not an unattractive one, in that no consideration is needed of the "correct" data interval, and also in that the possibility of very frequent (instantaneous) adjustments of advertising strategies are allowed. Continuous-time models can be discretized for estimation of model parameters from market data, so that such models do not provide a hindrance to empirical work. Models involving competition in continuous time are typically treated as *differen-*

tial games, in that critical state variables (e.g., sales, market share) are assumed to change with respect to time according to specified differential equations. A key consideration in any dynamic model of advertising competition involves how the advertising strategies of the competitors affect the differential process governing the changes in the sales or market-share state variables. As we shall see, a variety of models have been proposed.

The concept of a Nash equilibrium can be used to develop competing advertising strategies. In a differential game framework, however, this is not such a straightforward step. There are two general kinds of Nash equilibria that can be pursued: *open-loop*, in which advertising is a function only of time, and *closed-loop* equilibria, which define advertising to be a function not only of time but also the current state of the system. For closed-loop equilibria, current values of the state variables are used to summarize the current state. (As Clemhout and Wan (1979) indicate, there is some controversy as to whether the state variables should be considered adequate for defining closed-loop solutions.) More specifically, if X represents values of the state variables, t indicates time, and A_i denotes the advertising strategy for a particular competitor i, a function of time only, $A_i(t)$, indicates an open-loop strategy, while a function $A_i(X, t)$ is a closed-loop strategy.

Open-loop strategies are such that competitors commit at the outset to particular time paths of advertising expenditures. An open-loop Nash equilibrium is *time consistent* (Fershtman 1987a), in that if the players are asked at an intermediate point to reconsider their strategies they will not change them. However, if commitments at the outset are not feasible, and if an open-loop equilibrium depends on initial conditions, the initial values of the state variables X, the equilibrium is not *subgame perfect* (Fershtman 1987a, b); that is, the open-loop equilibrium does not constitute an equilibrium for a subgame that begins at a different position. The same reasoning holds for a closed-loop equilibrium that depends on initial values of the state variables. To be subgame perfect, an equilibrium must be free of dependence on initial conditions. Specifically, a strategy $A_i(X, t)$ that does not depend on initial conditions is termed a *feedback* strategy (Fershtman 1987b).

Open-loop and closed-loop equilibrium strategies are generally different (Jørgensen 1982a). By far the most frequently used approach has been to develop open-loop equilibria, primarily because they are easier to compute (Case 1979). In differential games, as opposed to optimal control problems which involve only a single decision-maker, closed-loop solutions usually involve a system of partial differential equations, which at best are very difficult to solve (Starr and Ho 1969).

The critical deficiency of open-loop strategies is precisely that, once determined, they are fixed. Open-loop strategies cannot be modified on the basis of, say, current market share. Marketing managers, however, are not likely to put their advertising strategies on "automatic pilot," and ignore inevitable and ongoing challenges to their market positions. Anecdotal examples abound of companies and brands responding to competitive threats to their market shares. Anheuser-Busch vs. Miller in the beer industry (*Business Week* 1982) is but one example. The "cola war" involving Coca-Cola vs. Pepsi-Cola (Morris 1987) provides another. See Kotler (1988, pp. 321–322), for further examples. Closed-loop equilibria, on the other hand, do allow strategies to adjust to the current state of the market, and as such as more realistic than open-loop strategies. It should be pointed out, however, that even closed-loop equilibria in differential game settings may not adequately represent certain dynamic aspects of markets, e.g., the ability of competitors to condition their actions on the past behavior of their rivals (Fershtman 1987a).

The difficulty in computing closed-loop solutions will undoubtedly retard general development in the area of differential games. There is hope for progress, however, in an approach suggested by Case (1979), in which he defines equilibrium strategies to be stationary (time-invariant) functions of state variables; advertising $A_i(X)$ is presumed to vary with the current state of the system, but not otherwise with time. The assumption of stationarity is not particularly limiting, however, since advertising strategies can vary with time as the state variables do. The critical and attractive feature of Case's approach is in the ongoing dependence on the state of the system. For a differential game involving a single state variable, the approach results in a system of ordinary, rather than partial, differential equations. Thus, for a limited but important class of problems, we have the ability to study advertising strategies that are dependent on the changing state of the market. We will use Case's approach as the basis for analytical derivations in subsequent chapters, and will outline the approach later in the present chapter.

Previous Research

Jørgensen (1982a) provides a review of early studies involving advertising competition in a differential game framework. We will review the highlights of those early modeling efforts, and will in addition review research that has been conducted since the Jørgensen survey.

As Jørgensen (1982a) indicates, while a variety of models have been studied, two important general models in particular attracted attention in early studies: the *Vidale–Wolfe* model and the *Lanchester* model. The Vidale–Wolfe model is a sales-response model developed originally by Vidale and Wolfe (1957) for a monopolistic firm. For sales rate S and advertising rate A, the Vidale–Wolfe model can be expressed as follows:

$$\dot{S} = \frac{dS}{dt} = f(A)(N - S) - \delta S \qquad (2.1)$$

where N is the maximum sales potential and δ is a decay parameter. (The notation is specific to this monograph for the sake of consistency.) The sales-response function is presented as a differential equation and exhibits elements of both growth and decay. Advertising affects only the untapped portion $(N - S)$.

The Lanchester model developed from a variation on Lanchester's formulation of the problem of combat recognized by Kimball (1957). The model is best expressed as changes to market share M:

$$\dot{M} = \frac{dM}{dt} = f_1(A_1)(1 - M) - f_2(A_2)M \qquad (2.2)$$

where A_1, A_2 are the advertising levels of two competitors in a duopoly, and M is competitor 1's market share. The Lanchester model is based upon the principle that the function of advertising in a competitive market is to attract the competitor's customers and sales to one's own product.

The Vidale–Wolfe and Lanchester models are really quite similar, in that the latter can be interpreted as a competitive generalization of the former (Little 1979). Model (2.2) can be derived by assuming rival sales to be equal to $N - S$, dividing equation (2.1) through by N, and making δ a function of rival advertising. The decay in a firm's sales/market share is seen as deriving from the advertising efforts of the firm's competitor. While the Vidale–Wolfe model is basically monopolistic, the Lanchester model would seem to be a logical extension for analysis of advertising competition.

Performance indices for the competitors (what they wish to maximize) vary somewhat across studies, but are of the following general type, for a duopoly:

$$J_i = \int_0^T g_i(S_1, S_2, A_1, A_2, t)dt + h_i(S_1(T), T), \ i = 1, 2. \qquad (2.3)$$

The profit rates, g_i, can be functions of the sales-rate state variables S_1, S_2, the advertising-rate variables A_1, A_2, and the time that has elapsed since the beginning of the planning horizon. For models working with market shares, only a single state variable is needed (as is also the case if $S_1 + S_2 = S$, a constant value). The h_i are salvage values that can depend on the ending sales values of the state variables and the length of the planning horizon. In some cases, T is assumed to be infinitely large.

For a duopoly, finding either open-loop or closed-loop solutions requires the definition of *Hamiltonians*:

$$H_i = g_i(S_1, S_2, A_1, A_2) + k_{i1}\dot{S}_1 + k_{i2}\dot{S}_2, \, i = 1, 2. \tag{2.4}$$

The k_{i1}, k_{i2} variables are so-called *costate* variables. Necessary conditions for an interior solution are that

$$\frac{\partial H_i}{\partial A_i} = 0, \, i = 1, 2 \tag{2.5}$$

and that the costate variables are subject to the following:

$$\dot{k}_{11} = -\frac{\partial H_1}{\partial S_1} - \frac{\partial H_1}{\partial A_2}\frac{\partial A_2^*}{\partial S_1}, \, k_{11}(T) = \frac{\partial h_1}{\partial S_1(T)}$$

$$\dot{k}_{12} = -\frac{\partial H_1}{\partial S_2} - \frac{\partial H_1}{\partial A_2}\frac{\partial A_2^*}{\partial S_2}, \, k_{12}(T) = \frac{\partial h_1}{\partial S_2(T)}$$

$$\dot{k}_{21} = -\frac{\partial H_2}{\partial S_1} - \frac{\partial H_2}{\partial A_1}\frac{\partial A_1^*}{\partial S_1}, \, k_{21}(T) = \frac{\partial h_2}{\partial S_1(T)}$$

$$\dot{k}_{22} = -\frac{\partial H_2}{\partial S_2} - \frac{\partial H_2}{\partial A_1}\frac{\partial A_1^*}{\partial S_2}, \, k_{22}(T) = \frac{\partial h_2}{\partial S_2(T)} \tag{2.6}$$

where A_1^* maximizes H_1 and A_2^* maximizes H_2. In addition, other constraints (e.g., a budget constraint) could be taken into account through a Lagrangian formulation. For open-loop solutions, the second term in each equation in (2.6) vanishes, since advertising strategies are presumed not to depend on the state variables; the problem becomes easier to solve, because only ordinary and not partial differentiation equations are involved.

The earliest differential game studies of advertising competition consider variations of the Vidale–Wolfe model. In an example to illustrate certain numerical algorithms, Mukundan and Elsner (1975) use the following duopoly model of sales change:

$$\dot{S}_i = \beta_i A_i \left(1 - \frac{S_i}{S_1 + S_2}\right) - \delta_i S_i, \, i = 1, 2. \tag{2.7}$$

Total industry sales $S_1 + S_2$ are not fixed. A shortcoming of the Mukundan and Elsner model (2.7) is that a firm's change in sales is not affected by the advertising of its rival.

For performance indices, Mukundan and Elsner assume the following as cost functionals, to be minimized:

$$J_i = \frac{1}{2} \int_0^T (B_i A_i^2 - D_i S_i^2) dt, \; i = 1, 2. \tag{2.8}$$

Admitting the difficulty in obtaining general closed-loop solutions, Mukundan and Elsner pursue *linear feedback* solutions, assuming that advertising levels of the two competitors respond in a linear fashion to sales values:

$$A_i = g_i[c_i S_i + (1 - c_i) S_{3-i}], \; i = 1, 2. \tag{2.9}$$

The g_i are parameters that can vary across time (and are not the same as the functions defined in equation (2.3)). Open-loop strategies are also calculated numerically for comparison.

Figure 2.1 shows open-loop and linear-feedback advertising levels for a particular set of problem parameters. Of interest is the open-loop solution in the early part of the planning period, when the advertising levels of the two firms are moving in opposite directions. The starting value for S_1 is 2.0 versus 1.0 for S_2. Otherwise, the two competitors have exactly the same parameter values. Apparently, an adjustment takes place in the early part of the period; firm 1's sales are too high and firm 2's too low, for symmetric competitors, and advertising is used dynamically to adjust these sales levels toward equal values. Eventually, the two advertising paths converge and decline toward zero (which is inevitable, since there is no salvage value in the model—there is no value to having a positive sales level at the end of the period). The linear feedback advertising levels, the behavior of which depends on the initial sales levels and the relationship in equation (2.9), are quite different from the open-loop values. The closed-loop levels proceed in opposite directions for the two firms, but here firm 1's advertising begins high and declines, while firm 2's starts low and increases. The expenditure paths cross, and neither is close to zero at the end of the planning period. Finally, it is calculated that both firms would be better off (would have lower cost) if they both adopted the open-loop strategies shown.

Deal (1979) numerically analyzes a somewhat different version of the Vidale–Wolfe model, but also one in which rival advertising has no assumed effect on a firm's sales change; see also the generalization of

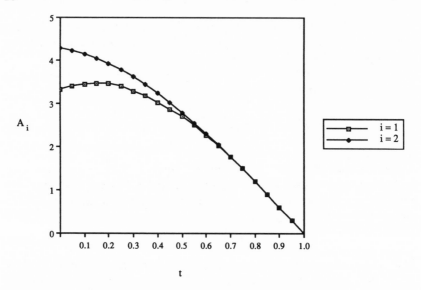

Figure 2.1a.   Open-Loop Equilibrium Strategies. Reproduced from Mukundan and Elsner (1975).

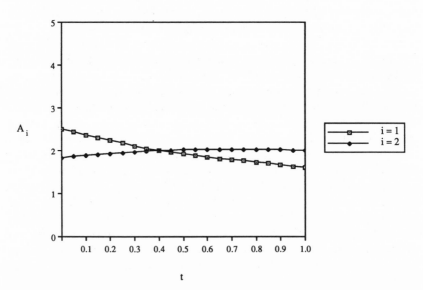

Figure 2.1b.   Linear Feedback Equilibrium Strategies. Reproduced from Mukundan and Elsner (1975).

Deal's model by Jones (1983), who does not study advertising dynamics but assumes steady-state advertising policies to investigate hysteresis in sales levels. In the Deal model, the sales dynamics are as follows

$$\dot{S}_i = \beta_i A_i \frac{N - S_1 - S_2}{N} - \delta_i S_i, \ i = 1, 2. \tag{2.10}$$

Deal includes squared advertising terms, to reflect convex advertising costs, and a salvage term in each of his performance indices:

$$J_i = \int_0^T (c_i S_i - A_i^2)dt + \frac{w_i S_i(T)}{S_1(T) + S_2(T)}, \ i = 1, 2. \tag{2.11}$$

The w_i parameters are weights reflecting the importance to the firms of terminal market share. The integral term measures the total (undiscounted) profits over the planning period. Deal is interested in two particular implications of the model (2.10)–(2.11): 1) the effect of differing values of the decay parameter δ_i (across the two competitors) on the open-loop advertising paths; and 2) the effect of differing values of the weights w_i on the advertising paths. Specifically, Deal hypothesizes regarding point 1 that the firm with a smaller decay parameter will be encouraged to advertise more, especially early in the planning period. With regard to point 2, the firm with the higher weighting of terminal market share will be encouraged to advertise more late in the planning period.

Numerical analysis of the model confirms Deal's conjectures. Figure 2.2 shows advertising paths for the two firms where $\delta_1 = .01$ and $\delta_2 = .25$; all other parameters are the same for the two competitors. Note that firm 1 advertises heavily early in the period and steadily decreases its advertising, crossing below firm 2's advertising path. Firm 2's advertising also shows decline over the planning period, but at a much slower rate.

The results shown in figure 2.3 confirm the second hypothesis regarding weighting of terminal market share. Firm 1's weight is set at $w_1 = 0.05N$ in the example shown, and firm 2's weight is set at a higher level, $w_2 = 1.50N$. Notice that not only is firm 2's advertising path at a higher level than firm 1's, but also firm 2's path turns up in the latter part of the planning period. That is, open-loop advertising declines to a low value only if the firm has set a low (or zero, as is the case in the Mukundan and Elsner (1975) model) value on its sales existing at the end of the planning horizon.

Case (1979) offers an early analysis of a Lanchester model, as an illustration of his development of *perfect equilibrium* strategies, which are functions of state variables. The following Lanchester structure is used to model dynamic changes in market share:

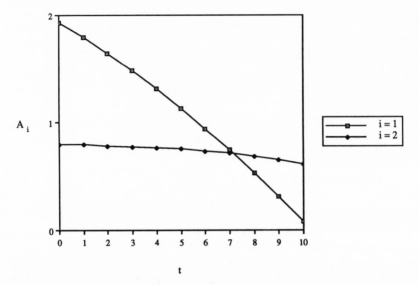

Figure 2.2. Open-Loop Equilibrium Strategies with Differing Decay Parameters. Reprinted with permission from *Operations Research*, 7(4), 1979, © 1979, Operations Research Society of America. No further reproduction permitted without the consent of the copyright owner.

$$\dot{M} = A_1(1 - M) - \alpha A_2 M \qquad (2.12)$$

where M is the market share of competitor 1. (Case (1975) considers an alternative form of the model.) As opposed to the Vidale–Wolfe models of Mukundan and Elsner (1975) and Deal (1979), the Lanchester model adopted by Case assumes that a firm's market share and therefore sales performance is affected directly not only by the firm's own advertising but also by that of its rival. Note that the advertising effects are assumed to be directly proportional to advertising levels, a simplified version of model (2.2). The performance indices involve discounted profits:

$$J_1 = \int_0^\infty e^{-\rho t}(PM - A_1^2)dt$$

$$J_2 = \int_0^\infty e^{-\rho t}[Q(1 - M) - A_2^2]dt. \qquad (2.13)$$

Note that an infinite planning horizon is assumed.

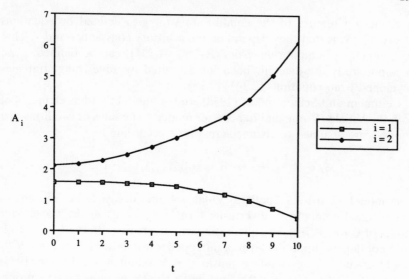

Figure 2.3. Open-Loop Equilibrium Strategies with Differing Terminal Weights. Reprinted with permission from *Operations Research*, 7(4), 1979, © 1979, Operations Research Society of America. No further reproduction permitted without the consent of the copyright owner.

Case is concerned not with open-loop solutions but with advertising strategies that vary with market share M. To find equilibrium strategies, Hamilton–Jacobi equations are manipulated to produce a system of ordinary differential equations in standard form. If $\rho = 0$, the equilibria are easily determined. If we define

$$B = \frac{\alpha M}{1 - M}$$

$$C = PM + 2c$$

$$D = Q(1 - M) + 2\gamma \qquad (2.14)$$

where c and γ are arbitrary constants, the equilibria may be expressed as follows:

$$A_1(M) = \frac{1}{\sqrt{3}}[2DB^2 - C + 2(D^2B^4 - CDB^2 + C^2)^{1/2}]^{1/2}$$

$$A_2(M) = \frac{1}{\sqrt{3}}\left[\frac{2C}{B^2} - D + 2\left(\frac{C^2}{B^4} - \frac{CD}{B^2} + D^2\right)^{1/2}\right]^{1/2}. \qquad (2.15)$$

A significant feature of the equilibrium strategies defined by equations (2.14)–(2.15) is that they depend on the arbitrary constants c and γ. That is, a number of equilibrium pairs $(A_1(M), A_2(M))$ can be defined. Case does not study the dynamic behavior exhibited by advertising strategies developed from equations (2.14)–(2.15).

Leitmann and Schmitendorf (1978) study a model that has elements of both the Vidale–Wolfe and Lanchester models. The sales of two firms in a duopoly are assumed to change across time according to

$$\dot{S}_i = A_i - \frac{c_i A_i^2}{2} - \delta_i S_i - \beta_i A_{3-i} S_i, \; i = 1, 2. \tag{2.16}$$

The model (2.16) has both a Vidale–Wolfe decay term $\delta_i S_i$ and a proportional competitor advertising term $\beta_i A_{3-i} S_i$ as in the Lanchester model of Case (1979). The quadratic own-advertising effect, $A_i - c_i A_i^2/2$, does not depend upon the level of untapped sales, as does the Case (1979) model or the Vidale–Wolfe extensions of Mukundan and Elsner (1975) and Deal (1979). The performance indices involve undiscounted profits and no salvage term:

$$J_i = \int_0^T (p_i S_i - A_i) dt, \; i = 1, 2. \tag{2.17}$$

Analysis of the model (2.16)–(2.17) shows that there is some terminal interval $[\hat{t}, T]$ on which the open-loop equilibrium advertising rates are both zero, which is not surprising given the lack of a salvage value. Furthermore, Leitmann and Schmitendorf establish that, for their model, the open-loop equilibria are also closed-loop strategies. (In general, models for which open-loop equilibria are also closed-loop would appear to offer analytical advantages due to their tractability. However, only restricted model structures yield such equilibria. See, for example, Clemhout and Wan (1979) and the discussion in Dockner, Feichtinger, and Jørgensen (1985) and Fershtman (1987b).)

Feichtinger (1983) studies a generalized version of the Leitmann and Schmitendorf (1978) model:

$$\dot{S} = g_i(A_i) - \delta_i S_i - k_i(A_{3-i}) S_i, \; i = 1, 2. \tag{2.18}$$

The advertising effectiveness functions $g_i(A_i)$ are assumed to be concave, while functions measuring the effectiveness of rival advertising $k_i(A_{3-i})$ are assumed to be increasing in rival advertising expenditures. The performance indices assumed by Feichtinger involve discounted profits and salvage terms:

$$J_i = \int_0^T e^{-r_it}(q_iS_i - A_i)dt + e^{-r_iT}w_iS_i(T), \; i = 1, 2. \qquad (2.19)$$

Feichtinger provides a qualitative analysis of the generalized model and, in particular, finds conditions under which a unique stationary point exists in the interior of the admissible region of the Nash-solution advertising controls.

Models simpler in structure than either the Lanchester or the Vidale–Wolfe model have also been studied. Olsder (1976) poses the following *excess advertising* model, in which it is assumed that sales flow in the direction of the firm that advertises in the excess:

$$\dot{S}_i = A_i - A_{3-i}, \; i = 1, 2. \qquad (2.20)$$

Total sales are constrained to equal one ($S_1 + S_2 = 1$). As is seen in equation (2.20), the greater the excess in advertising, the greater the flow in sales from one competitor to the other. This model may be appropriate in situations in which customers lack loyalty and change brands simply on the basis of which brand advertises more. An additional reason for reviewing the excess advertising model is that subsequent studies combine such effects with Vidale–Wolfe and Lanchester aspects.

The performance indices adopted by Olsder are

$$J_i = \int_0^T (c_iS_i - A_i)dt, \; i = 1, 2. \qquad (2.21)$$

The following constraints are initially imposed:

$$A_i \geq 0, \; i = 1, 2$$
$$A_i \leq c_iS_i, \; i = 1, 2. \qquad (2.22)$$

The latter of these constraints indicates that all advertising expenditures are internally financed. Defining

$$\bar{A}_i = \frac{A_i}{S_i}, \; i = 1, 2 \qquad (2.23)$$

the open-loop solution to the problem (2.20)–(2.22), which also happens to be the closed-loop solution, is

$$\bar{A}_i = c_i, \; 0 \leq t \leq t_i, \; = 0, \; t_i \leq t \leq T, \; i = 1, 2 \qquad (2.24)$$

where, if $c_1 \geq c_2$,

$$t_1 = T - \frac{1}{c_1}$$

$$t_2 = t_1 - \ln \frac{c_1(1 + c_2)}{c_2(1 + c_1)}. \tag{2.25}$$

The bang-bang nature of the solution is due to the linearity in the system.

If the following constraints are added

$$S_i \geq 0, \; i = 1, 2 \tag{2.26}$$

the solution in equations (2.24)–(2.25) is only a candidate. Other possibilities are *bankrupt-policies*, in which one of the competitors, say firm 1, sets $\bar{A}_1 = 0$, and the other firm sets $\bar{A}_2 = 1$ until firm 1 has no customers, and then sets $\bar{A}_2 = 0$. If for one of the firms the bankrupt-policy compares favorably, in terms of profit, to equations (2.24)–(2.25), the bankrupt-policy is the solution. Whether bankrupt-policies or the solutions (2.24)–(2.25) are adopted, advertising levels of both competitors are reduced to zero by the end of the planning horizon. This result is consistent with other studies involving no salvage value, Mukundan and Elsner (1975) and Leitmann and Schmitendorf (1978).

Jørgensen (1982b) imposes nonlinearities on the Olsder (1976) model:

$$\dot{S}_i = k \log \frac{A_i}{A_{3-i}} = k(\log A_i - \log A_{3-i}), \; i = 1, 2. \tag{2.27}$$

Total sales are assumed fixed. For performance indices, Jørgensen assumes discounted profits:

$$J_i = \int_0^T e^{-r_i t}(q_i S_i - A_i)dt, \; i = 1, 2. \tag{2.28}$$

Analysis of the model (2.27)–(2.28) shows that open-loop advertising strategies decline exponentially to zero. That advertising declines to zero, of course, is to be expected, given no salvage value on sales.

Feichtinger and Dockner (1984) further generalize the excess advertising model, and assume

$$\dot{S}_1 = g(A_1, A_2) \tag{2.29}$$

where

$$\frac{\partial g}{\partial A_1} > 0, \frac{\partial^2 g}{\partial A_1^2} < 0,$$

$$\frac{\partial g}{\partial A_2} < 0, \frac{\partial^2 g}{\partial A_2^2} > 0. \tag{2.30}$$

Conditions leading to monotonic decline in open-loop advertising expenditures are explored. A basic condition is that salvage values are equal to zero. If in addition it is assumed that $\partial^2 g/\partial A_1 \partial A_2 \leq 0$ (Feichtinger and Dockner interpret this as meaning that firm 1 is the market leader, in that a rise in firm 1's advertising may increase the marginal efficiency of firm 2's advertising, while an increase in firm 2's spending will not increase firm 1's advertising efficiency), the authors show that firm 2's open-loop advertising decreases monotonically, while that of firm 1 cannot be determined. If $\partial^2 g/\partial A_1 \partial A_2 = 0$, however, the open-loop strategies for both firms show monotonic decline, which is consistent with Jørgensen's result (Jørgensen 1982b). Other restrictions also lead to monotonic decline in advertising for both firms.

Deal, Sethi, and Thompson (1979) provide a model that combines Vidale–Wolfe and excess advertising effects:

$$\dot{S}_i = \beta_i A_i (1 - S_1 - S_2) - \delta_i S_i + e_i (A_i - A_{3-i})(S_1 + S_2), i = 1, 2. \tag{2.31}$$

The performance indices involve discounted profits as well as a salvage term:

$$J_i = \int_0^T e^{-\rho t}(c_i S_i - A_i^2)dt + w_i e^{-\rho T} S_i(T), i = 1, 2. \tag{2.32}$$

Open-loop equilibria are determined numerically. The authors are interested primarily in the effects on competitive advertising of three parameters: the decay parameter δ_i, the weight on terminal sales w_i, and the excess advertising parameter e_i. Various competitive encounters are analyzed, in which the three parameters are varied; all other parameters remain fixed and equal for the two competitors. Certain results are similar to those obtained by Deal (1979). That is, the firm with the lower decay-parameter value spends more on advertising early in the planning period. Also, a heavy weight on terminal sales encourages a pattern of growing advertising near the end of the planning period. In contrast, advertising declines toward zero if a weight of zero is placed on terminal sales, a result consistent with those from Vidale–Wolfe (Mukundan and Elsner 1975; Leitmann and Schmitendorf 1978) and excess-advertising (Olsder 1976; Jørgensen 1982b; Feichtinger and Dockner 1984) extensions that involve zero salvage values. The unique aspect of the Deal, Sethi, and Thompson model is in the excess-advertising effect. Figure 2.4 shows the advertising

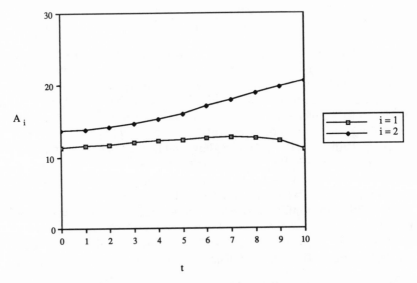

Figure 2.4. Open-Loop Equilibrium Strategies with Differing Excess Advertising Effects. Reprinted from Deal, Sethi, and Thompson (1979), p. 107, by courtesy of Marcel Dekker, Inc.

paths of the two firms when $e_1 = .01$ and $e_2 = .02$ (and w_i as at a fairly large value). Not surprisingly, the firm with the greater ability to attract sales through heavier advertising (firm 2) tends to spend more on advertising.

Sorger (1989) analyzes the following modification of the Lanchester model of market-share adjustment:

$$\dot{M} = A_1\sqrt{1 - M} - A_2\sqrt{M}. \tag{2.33}$$

Sorger argues that the formulation in equation (2.33) can be interpreted as combining Lanchester dynamics with an excess advertising interpretation. This is because the square roots $\sqrt{1 - M}$ and $\sqrt{M}$ can be approximated by the quadratic expressions $1 - M + M(1 - M)$ and $M + M(1 - M)$, respectively. Applying this approximation to equation (2.33) yields

$$\dot{M} = A_1(1 - M) - A_2M + (A_1 - A_2)M(1 - M). \tag{2.34}$$

The first two terms on the right-hand side of equation (2.34) form a simple Lanchester model, while the last term provides the excess advertising element, which combines the difference in advertising with the contact rate $M(1 - M)$ between customers of the two firms. Sorger's performance indices involve discounted profits and salvage terms:

$$J_1 = \int_0^T e^{-r_1 t}\left(q_1 M - \frac{c_1}{2}A_1^2\right)dt + e^{-r_1 T}w_1 M(T)$$

$$J_2 = \int_0^T e^{-r_2 t}\left(q_2(1 - M) - \frac{c_2}{2}A_2^2\right)dt + e^{-r_2 T}w_2[1 - M(T)]. \quad (2.35)$$

Sorger's model is especially interesting in that a feedback equilibrium can be determined explicitly. Sorger performs a qualitative analysis on the feedback equilibrium as well as the unique open-loop solution for the problem (2.33, 2.35), noting that the two solutions have similar structure. One particular finding of interest is that the equilibrium advertising of a firm tends to be high when the firm's market share is low, and vice versa, indicating that advertising may be used to adjust market share toward a more desired level, a phenomenon indicated in the open-loop, if not the feedback, strategies of Mukundan and Elsner (1975).

Recent years have seen the marketing literature become interested in differential game modeling of advertising competition. In particular, the Lanchester model is the foundation for the study by Erickson (1985), who analyzes the following version of the model:

$$\dot{M} = \beta_{12}A_1^{\alpha_1}(1 - M) - \beta_{21}A_2^{\alpha_2}M. \quad (2.36)$$

The power function relationships in equation (2.36) are included in the model to allow for advertising effects that diminish as advertising expenditures increase. Discounted profits are used as performance indices for the duopolistic competitors:

$$J_1 = \int_0^T e^{-rt}(g_1 MS - A_1)dt$$

$$J_2 = \int_0^T e^{-rt}[g_2(1 - M)S - A_2]dt \quad (2.37)$$

where S represents total industry sales. Erickson is interested in the steady-state behavior of competitive advertising, as well as how advertising behaves dynamically outside of steady state. Steady-state analysis of open-loop equilibria, where $\dot{M} = \dot{A}_1 = \dot{A}_2 = 0$, reveals that relative advertising is related to parameters of the problem in the following manner:

$$\frac{A_1}{A_2} = \frac{g_1 \alpha_1}{g_2 \alpha_2}. \quad (2.38)$$

If the elasticities α_1, α_2 are equal, then relative advertising in steady state depends only upon the relative values of the unit contributions of the two competitors

$$\frac{A_1}{A_2} = \frac{g_1}{g_2} \qquad (2.39)$$

and relative market shares in steady state depend on the relative unit contributions as well as on the relative values of the advertising effectiveness parameters

$$\frac{M}{1-M} = \frac{\beta_{12}g_1}{\beta_{21}g_2}. \qquad (2.40)$$

Tang (1990) offers a generalization of these results to a general number of competitors.

To gain insight regarding the dynamic movement of advertising out of steady state, Erickson conducts numerical analyses of open-loop equilibria, assuming a more general model that allows for market expansion.

$$\dot{S}_i = \beta_{i,3-i}A_i^{\alpha_i}S_{3-i} - \beta_{3-i,i}A_{3-i}^{\alpha_{3-i}}S_i + \beta_i A_i^{\alpha_i}e, \ i = 1, 2 \qquad (2.41)$$

where e is a market-expansion parameter ranging from zero to one in the numerical analyses. A value $e = 0$ implies that no market expansion is possible, and advertising serves only to adjust the market shares of the two competitors. Two general types of patterns develop, as shown in figures 2.5 and 2.6. The most frequent pattern is shown in figure 2.5 and shows the advertising paths of the two competitors proceeding in opposite directions. This pattern is interpreted as one of adjustment of relative sales levels, similar to the adjustment phenomena detected in the open-loop numerical result of Mukundan and Elsner (1975) and the qualitative analysis of Sorger (1989). The other general pattern, shown in figure 2.6, of increasing advertising on the part of both competitors, occurs in 10% of the simulations and is associated with high values of the market-expansion parameter e. When the ability to expand the total market is at a high level, both competitors expand advertising over time to take advantage of this ability. As figure 2.5 indicates, on the other hand, when market expansion is limited and the competition is for market share of a stable market, initial advertising levels are set to begin a process of adjustment of undesirable market share levels, and the advertising levels of the two competitors then proceed in opposite directions toward desirable steady-state levels of advertising and market share.

In marketing, a popular model of sales growth has been the *diffusion* model, emanating from Bass (1969b):

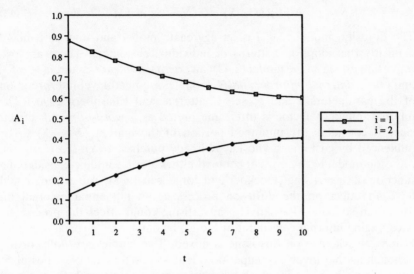

Figure 2.5.   Open-Loop Equilibrium Advertising Strategies to Adjust Sales Levels.
Based on the model from Erickson (1985).

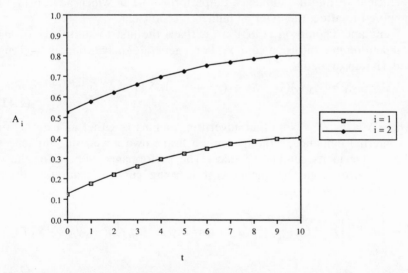

Figure 2.6.   Open-Loop Equilibrium Advertising Strategies to Expand Market.
Based on the model from Erickson (1985).

$$\dot{S} = (a + bS)(N - S) = a(N - S) + bS(N - S). \qquad (2.42)$$

The diffusion model (2.42) is an aggregate model and does not model explicitly the adoption patterns of individual customers. There are two important effects in the model (2.42): an *external influence* factor, $a(N - S)$, and one of *internal influence*, $bS(N - S)$. (For a microlevel interpretation of the parameters a and b, see Chatterjee and Eliashberg 1990.) The internal influence factor is often interpreted as a *word-of-mouth* effect, since it considers the untapped portion of the market $(N - S)$ to be influenced by customers who have already purchased (S). To relate the diffusion model to the present context, either a or b could be considered a function of advertising (Dockner and Jørgensen 1988). Advertising could have an effect on the diffusion process as an influential external in-formation source. Alternatively, advertising could affect the process by encouraging internal considerations, e.g., by emphasizing social pressure. Empirical evidence on this issue is mixed. Two studies are noteworthy, although neither involves competition. Horsky and Simon (1983) postulate and validate a model in which advertising acts only through the external influence factor. On the other hand, Simon and Sebastion (1987), noting contextual realities, find that a model in which advertising influences the coefficient of internal influence outperforms one in which advertising is supposed to affect the external influence coefficient.

Teng and Thompson (1983) are perhaps the first to study advertising competition in a diffusion context. For a general n-player oligopoly, Teng and Thompson define

$$\dot{S}_i = (\gamma_{i1} + \gamma_{i2}A_i)(1 - S) + (\gamma_{i3} + \gamma_{i4}A_i)S_i(1 - S), i = 1, \ldots, n \qquad (2.43)$$

where $S = \sum_{i=1}^{n} S_i$. Note that advertising can act as either an external or an internal influence, although only a firm's own advertising influences the change in its cumulative sales. The performance indices for the n players incorporate production-cost learning curves, quadratic adver-tising costs, and salvage values:

$$J_i = \int_0^T e^{-\rho_i t}\left\{\left[p_i - C_{i0}\left(\frac{S_{i0}}{S_i}\right)^{e_i}\right]\dot{S}_i - (\alpha_i A_i^2 + \beta_i A_i + \delta_i)\right\}dt + W_i e^{-\rho_i T}S_i(T),$$

$$i = 1, \ldots, n \qquad (2.44)$$

where p_i is a constant (across time) price. (Thompson and Teng (1984) study both price and advertising as decision variables.) A numerical algor-ithm is used to obtain open-loop solutions. For duopoly problems ($n = 2$),

Teng and Thompson find that, ceteris paribus, a firm's advertising level will increase with increases in the following parameters: W_i, γ_{i2}, γ_{i4}, e_i, p_i. Increases in the following parameters will lead to a decrease in advertising: γ_{i1}, γ_{i3}, C_{i0}, a_i, where $a_i = \alpha_i A_i^2 + \beta_i A_i + \delta_i$.

Teng and Thompson also study various triopoly ($n = 3$) problems, numerically. One result they note is that higher values of the learning parameters e_i across firms lead to higher advertising levels. In addition, Teng and Thompson show that three different kinds of advertising paths can exist. In an example in which learning parameters, initial sales levels, and initial production costs vary across three competitors, the advertising for one firm remains positive for the entire planning period, approaching zero at the end, that of another rises from zero to become positive for a while before returning to zero, and the third firm does not advertise at all. A final conclusion is that advertising of each competing firm becomes zero when the market nears saturation ($\dot{S} = 0$). That is, competitive advertising eventually declines to zero, although the path may not be monotonic. It should be noted that the advertising decline occurs in the diffusion model not because of a zero or low salvage value, as in other models, but is due to the saturation of first-time sales; repeat sales are not included in the model.

A study of a diffusion model by Horsky and Mate (1988) is notable in that it analyzes closed-loop solutions exclusively. The modeling framework is different from other studies reviewed herein, in that the dynamic advertising competition and market development are not treated as a differential game, but as a *two-player Markov game*, which involves a discrete state space and uncertain transition between states. The transition probabilities are modeled as a diffusion process. Horsky and Mate define the state of the market as having two coordinates (x, y) where x equals the number of customers who have purchased firm 1's product and y equals the number of customers who have purchased the product of firm 2. Also, $z = m - x - y$ is the number of customers who yet to purchase from either firm. From (x, y), the market can move either to $(x + 1, y)$ or $(x, y + 1)$. The transition probabilities contain both advertising and word-of-mouth effects:

$$Pr(x + 1, y; t + dt \mid x, y; t) = (a_1 + w_1 x)z\, dt + o(dt)$$

$$Pr(x, y + 1; t + dt \mid x, y; t) = (a_2 + w_2 y)z\, dt + o(dt). \qquad (2.45)$$

Advertising is presumed to act only as an external influence, and advertising effectiveness a_i, $i = 1, 2$, is assumed to be a logarithmic function of firm i's advertising expenditures. Note that, as in Teng and Thompson (1983) as well as the Vidale–Wolfe extensions of Mukundan and Elsner (1975) and Deal (1979), rival advertising does not affect the change in a firm's state variable. Performance indices are expected present values of profit over an infinite time horizon.

Horsky and Mate pursue *stationary* advertising strategies, strategies that depend on the state of the market but not explicitly on time. Through numerical analysis of a specific example, which involves dynamic programming and iterative search, they determine that advertising expenditure rates decline as market penetration increases, a finding consistent with Teng and Thompson (1983). Further, Horsky and Mate analyze situations in which one of the firms has an early entrant advantage. They find that the late entrant should advertise at a greater rate than the early entrant, a result consistent with the evidence in Mukundan and Elsner (1975), Erickson (1985), and Sorger (1989) that firms with low market shares will tend to advertise at high levels, and vice versa, to adjust market shares to more desirable levels. Another result from Horsky and Mate is that the early entrant's advantage can only be overcome if the late entrant has a larger word-of-mouth parameter w_i.

Finally, Dockner and Jørgensen (1990) are able to obtain analytical results for certain constrained versions of a general diffusion model involving multiple competitors in a differential game framework. In particular, for a version that involves sales dynamics similar to those adopted by Horsky and Mate (1988) (but in continuous time and with a general number of competitors n)

$$\dot{S}_i = (a + b\ln A_i + dS)(N - S), \quad i = 1, \ldots, n \qquad (2.46)$$

where S is the sum of cumulative sales figures over all n competitors, Dockner and Jørgensen establish that the open-loop strategies of the competitors involve decreasing advertising rates, if no discounting and constant unit costs are assumed. Thus, Dockner and Jørgensen demonstrate that the basic result of declining competitive advertising for first-purchase-only diffusion models can be extended, under certain conditions, to a general number of competitors.

The primary focus of the present monograph is on differential game formulations in which sales or market shares are state variables that are influenced directly and dynamically through the advertising efforts of competing firms. Another approach has been to interpret advertising as affecting the *goodwill* of competitors, extending the model of Nerlove and Arrow (1962) to oligopolistic situations. Goodwill models define state variables in terms of advertising goodwill stocks, which in turn influence the sales of the competitors. Although goodwill models are not a primary focus, progress has been made in the area, which deserves at least brief mention. Starting with an assumption of uncertainty in the relationships involving advertising expenditures, goodwill, and sales, Tapiero (1979) formulates two differential games for a duopoly situation: a sales-maximization game, which is zero sum, and a profit-maximization game, which is nonzero sum. For the profit-maximization game, Tapiero examines qualitatively both open-loop and linear-feedback advertising strategies. Fershtman (1984) obtains some general results regarding open-loop stationary Nash equilibrium points in an n-firm model: 1) firms with lower production costs obtain larger market share; 2) as the number of firms increases, the firms' goodwill and advertising at the equilibrium point tend to decrease, except possibly for the market share leader and 3) if all firms are identical, the firms' goodwill and advertising tend to decrease as the interest rate, the depreciation rate, or the production cost increases. Fershtman's model assumes linear advertising costs. With a discrete-time model involving convex advertising costs, Rao (1984) establishes the existence of an open-loop Nash equilibrium. Further, Rao examines the stability of stationary equilibria. The studies by Tapiero (1979), Fershtman (1984), and Rao (1984) all involve advertising as the sole decision variable of each firm. Thépot (1983) combines advertising with price and investment decisions, and Friedman (1983) and Fershtman, Mahajan, and Muller (1990) consider output decisions jointly with advertising. In addition, Thépot (1983) studies the effects of growth and competition on open-loop advertising, pricing, and investment policies. Friedman (1983) obtains an open-loop Nash equilibrium for a symmetric model in which profit functions are quadratic in terms of goodwill and output. Finally, Fershtman, Mahajan, and Muller (1990) determine conditions under which asymmetries in initial production cost and accumulated goodwill do not lead to an ultimate market-share advantage. As a whole, solid contributions have been made in the extension of the Nerlove–Arrow goodwill model to a competitive setting, although additional extensions in certain directions, e.g., closed-loop equilibria, would be useful.

The accompanying table 2.1 lists the various studies reviewed.

Summary of Previous Findings

Research to date frequently has relied on numerical approaches to develop dynamic insights. Only certain model structures yield analytical or qualitative conclusions regarding the dynamic evolution of advertising competition. Dockner, Feichtinger, and Jørgensen (1985) discuss structural conditions that allow the solution of differential games. Analytical difficulties notwithstanding, reliance on numerical results limits the general usefulness of

Table 2.1.   Previous studies modeling advertising competition

Study	Model type	Solution type	Analysis method
Mukundan and Elsner (1975)	Vidale–Wolfe	Open-loop, linear feedback	Numerical
Deal (1979)	Vidale–Wolfe	Open-loop	Numerical
Case (1979)	Lanchester	Perfect	Analytical
Leitmann and Schmitendorf (1978)	Vidale–Wolfe/ Lanchester	Open-loop = closed-loop	Analytical
Feichtinger (1983)	Vidale–Wolfe/ Lanchester	Open-loop = closed-loop	Qualitative
Olsder (1976)	Excess advertising	Open-loop = closed-loop	Analytical
Jørgensen (1982b)	Excess advertising	Open-loop	Analytical
Feichtinger and Dockner (1984)	Excess advertising	Open-loop	Qualitative
Deal, Sethi, and Thompson (1979)	Vidale–Wolfe/ excess advertising	Open-loop	Numerical
Sorger (1989)	Lanchester/ excess advertising	Open-loop, feedback	Qualitative
Erickson (1985)	Lanchester	Open-loop	Analytical, numerical
Teng and Thompson (1983)	Diffusion	Open-loop	Numerical
Horsky and Mate (1988)	Diffusion	Closed-loop	Numerical
Dockner and Jørgensen (1990)	Diffusion	Open-loop	Analytical
Tapiero (1979)	Nerlove–Arrow	Open-loop, linear feedback	Qualitative
Fershtman (1984)	Nerlove–Arrow	Open-loop	Analytical
Rao (1984)	Nerlove–Arrow	Open-loop	Analytical
Thépot (1983)	Nerlove–Arrow	Open-loop	Qualitative
Friedman (1983)	Nerlove–Arrow	Open-loop	Analytical
Fershtman, Mahajan, and Muller (1990)	Nerlove–Arrow	Open-loop	Analytical

the findings. Still, some patterns appear that may aid our understanding of dynamic advertising in competitive markets. It should be recognized in interpreting the patterns that some results are for open-loop equilibria while others involve closed-loop solutions.

A frequent pattern that appears is that of advertising decreasing over time. While this pattern may be due to the dynamic structure assumed, as in the diffusion models of Teng and Thompson (1983), Horsky and Mate (1988), and Dockner and Jørgensen (1990), wherein advertising declines to zero as the market saturates, it is more frequently due simply to the assumption of a fixed horizon with no salvage value. Mukundan and Elsner (1975), Olsder (1976), Leitmann and Schmitendorf (1978), Jørgensen (1982b), and Feichtinger and Dockner (1984) all derive declining advertising implications from such a scenario. In addition, Deal (1979) finds declining advertising on the part of both competitors when a nonzero, but low, salvage value is assumed. As Deal (1979) and Deal, Sethi, and Thompson (1979) show, however, the weight put on the salvage value of market share makes a great deal of difference in the direction advertising takes as the end of the planning horizon is approached. It cannot be concluded that a pattern of declining advertising is a general phenomenon.

Most studies assume a fixed time horizon, although Case (1979) and Horsky and Mate (1988) view their problems in the framework of an infinite time horizon, and Feichtinger (1983) and Sorger (1989) consider an infinite as well as a finite time horizon. There are advantages to assuming a time horizon that stretches toward infinity. One advantage is that the problem of deciding what weight to put on the terminal market share or sales level is eliminated, since no salvage-value term is needed. Also, assuming an infinite horizon obviates the need to select an appropriate (finite) length of the planning horizon, an essentially arbitrary process. The boundary conditions provided by a salvage term in a finite-horizon problem can be replaced by those proceeding from the assumption that the system approaches a steady state (Kamien and Schwartz 1981). Viewing a dynamic problem as one that approaches a steady state offers the attractive prospect of observing how competitors use advertising to adjust beginning market shares or sales levels to desirable steady-state levels.

Even with finite time horizons, certain studies show evidence of advertising being used to adjust market shares or sales levels. Erickson (1985) notes this in a majority of his simulations (see figure 2.5). It is also evident in the open-loop solution of Mukundan and Elsner (1975) (figure 2.1). A disparity in share or sales relative to competition is adjusted for with a high and gradually decreasing level of advertising, if share or the sales level is too low initially, or low and increasing advertising, if share or sales level is too high. Further evidence of this adjustment phenomenon is provided by the conclusion of Sorger (1989) that firms with low market shares choose high advertising rates, and vice versa, and the finding by Horsky and Mate (1988) that a late entrant advertises at a higher level than the early entrant in a market, in an attempt to overcome its disadvantage.

In addition to the dynamics of the approach to steady state, it can also be interesting to study the nature of the steady state itself. Analysis can potentially characterize the steady-state advertising and sales or market-share levels, and, through comparative statics, determine the influence of model parameters on the steady state. Since a steady state describes the long-run nature of a competitive market situation, it would appear to be an especially important aspect to study. Existing research, however, has been interested primarily in the transitory aspect of advertising strategies, with some exceptions (Deal, Sethi, and Thompson 1979; Erickson 1985; Tang 1990).

Finally, closed-loop equilibria are underresearched. A far too frequent pattern in existing research has been to opt for the more tractable open-loop solutions. Except for particular models, as in Olsder (1976) or Leitmann and Schmitendorf (1978), where the structure is such that open-loop solutions are also closed-loop, closed-loop equilibria are likely to be different from open-loop equilibria. Additional study should indicate more fully the nature of closed-loop solutions as well as the extent of the differences between open-loop and closed-loop advertising strategies.

Models

It is the intention of the present study to extend existing research by analyzing closed-loop advertising strategies (more specifically, the perfect equilibria of Case (1979)) and to compare them with open-loop strategies. This will be done in the context of three basic models that have gained popularity in the literature on dynamic advertising competition: the *Lanchester*, *Vidale–Wolfe*, and *diffusion* models. For these models, closed-loop equilibria are in general different from open-loop strategies, although, as will be shown through examples, it is possible to find closed-loop strategies that resemble open-loop strategies, dynamically. We will restrict each model to involve a duopoly (two competitors) and a single state variable, to avoid partial differential equations.

The Lanchester model has been advanced as an attractive model that directly incorportes both competition and the dynamic nature of markets (Little 1979). An especially interesting feature is that the model, in steady state, yields a logically consistent "us/(us + them)" structure. The model is defined in terms of changes to firm 1's market share M:

$$\dot{M} = \beta_1 A_1^{\alpha_1}(1 - M) - \beta_2 A_2^{\alpha_2}M. \tag{2.47}$$

This is the same model as equation (2.36) (dropping the second subscripts on the β's), analyzed by Erickson (1985) in an open-loop framework. Power functions are used for the advertising effects to allow for non-linearity, specifically the diminishing marginal effects of advertising: $0 < \alpha_1, \alpha_2 < 1$. Also $\beta_1, \beta_2 > 0$. An infinite planning horizon is assumed for the performance indices of the two competitors:

$$J_1 = \int_0^\infty e^{-rt}(g_1 M - A_1)dt$$

$$J_2 = \int_0^\infty e^{-rt}[g_2(1 - M) - A_2]dt. \tag{2.48}$$

The parameters g_1 and g_2 represent the values of market share to competitors 1 and 2, respectively, and can be interpreted as unit contributions multiplied by the fixed total market size. The discount rate r is assumed to be equal for the two competitors.

The Vidale–Wolfe model has had a long history as a popular expression of dynamic advertising effects. Its basic form needs to be extended to incorporate competition. In the present formulation, the Vidale–Wolfe model is used to represent the evolution of *total industry sales S*:

$$\dot{S} = (\beta_1 A_1^{\alpha_1} + \beta_2 A_2^{\alpha_2})(N - S) - \delta S. \tag{2.49}$$

The advertising of each competitor acts nonlinearly to attract untapped sales to the market. Restrictions on $\alpha_1, \alpha_2, \beta_1, \beta_2$ are as above. Sales decay at a constant proportional rate of δ. As opposed to the Lanchester model (2.47), advertising in the Vidale–Wolfe model (2.49) is not used in direct competition for market share. Rather, each competitor's advertising is used in the attempt to attract total market sales S, which are then divided between the two competitors according to relative values of "brand-strength" parameters $\gamma_1, \gamma_2 > 0$. That is, the sales of firm $i = 1, 2$ are

$$S_i = \frac{\gamma_i}{\gamma_1 + \gamma_2} S, i = 1, 2. \tag{2.50}$$

The brand-strength parameters can be interpreted as being determined by factors not explicitly modeled and assumed to be fixed across time—e.g., a persistent brand image, distribution strength. This particular treatment of advertising competition in the context of the Vidale–Wolfe model is needed so that the model involves a single state variable. The performance indices for the two competitors are

$$J_i = \int_0^\infty e^{-rt}(h_i S_i - A_i)dt, \, i = 1, 2 \qquad (2.51)$$

where the h_i are unit contributions.

The diffusion model has gained popularity in the marketing literature as a useful basic model of first purchases of a new product (Mahajan, Muller, and Bass 1990). The desire in the present study is to interpret the diffusion model in a context of ongoing sales for duopolistic competitors. A Vidale–Wolfe-type decay term is combined with the basic diffusion model (2.42) to represent the evolution of *repeat* sales for the total industry:

$$\dot{S} = (\beta_1 A_1^{\alpha_1} + \beta_2 A_2^{\alpha_2} + \varepsilon S)(N - S) - \delta S. \qquad (2.52)$$

The relationship in equation (2.52) involves both a diffusion buildup, which depends on the advertising of both competitors as well as a word-of-mouth influence εS, and a Vidale–Wolfe decay. Advertising is assumed to affect only the innovation coefficient in the diffusion process. Like the Vidale–Wolfe model (2.49), advertising in equation (2.52) is used to attract total industry sales, which are then divided between the two competitors on the basis of brand-strength parameters γ_1, γ_2 as in equation (2.50). Also, preformance indices are as in equation (2.51).

Strategy Concepts

We wish to study, for comparative purposes, both open-loop and closed-loop solutions to the three models (Lanchester, Vidale–Wolfe, diffusion). The general approach to derivation of open-loop equilibria is well known and will not be repeated here (c.f. Jørgensen 1982a).

To derive closed-loop strategies, there are two approaches (Fershtman 1987a): 1) exploiting Pontryagin-type conditions (see also Jørgensen 1982a for description of such conditions) and 2) a value-function approach. Each approach involves, in general, a system of partial differential equations. The lack of a general theory of partial differential equations would seem to prevent study of closed-loop solutions.

Case (1979) offers a useful approach, however, at least for a set of problems. Case uses a value-function approach to develop what are termed *perfect equilibria.* The general approach is described in Case (1979, ch. 8). For simplicity of exposition, assume a duopoly and a single state variable X, which varies across time according to a general function involving current values of X and the advertising rates of the two competitors A_1 and A_2:

$$\dot{X} = f(X, A_1, A_2). \tag{2.53}$$

Also, assume the following performance indices for the two players:

$$J_i = \int_0^\infty e^{-rt} g_i(X, A_1, A_2) dt, \ i = 1, 2. \tag{2.54}$$

A *strategy* for competitor i is a function $A_i^*(X)$ that assigns a value for the advertising variable of player i to each value of X. A pair of strategies A_1^*, A_2^* is a *perfect equilibrium* if each of the implied performance indices J_1, J_2 is maximized over all possible strategies and for every starting value of X.

Case formally shows the validity of the following procedure. Define the Hamiltonians

$$H_i = g_i(X, A_1, A_2) + k_i f(X, A_1, A_2), \ i = 1, 2 \tag{2.55}$$

and determine, if possible, $\hat{A}_1(X, k_1, k_2)$ and $\hat{A}_2(X, k_1, k_2)$ that form a Nash equilibrium for the auxiliary game

$$i \max H_i, \ i = 1, 2. \tag{2.56}$$

Now define the *Hamilton–Jacobi* (or *Hamilton–Jacobi–Bellman*) equations

$$\begin{aligned} g_i(X, \hat{A}_1[X, V_1'(X), V_2'(x)], \hat{A}_2[X, V_1'(X), V_2'(X)]) \\ + V_i'(X) f(X, \hat{A}_1[X, V_1'(X), V_2'(X), \hat{A}_2(X, V_1'(X), V_2'(X)]) \\ = rV_i(X) + c_i, \ i = 1, 2 \end{aligned} \tag{2.57}$$

where the c_i are arbitary real constants. The functions $V_i(X)$ are termed *value functions*. If the system of equations (2.57) can be solved for $V_1(X)$ and $V_2(X)$, a perfect equilibrium is derived through the following relationships:

$$A_i^*(X) = \hat{A}_i[X, V_1'(X), V_2'(X)], \ i = 1, 2. \tag{2.58}$$

It is important to note that, with a single state variable, the system (2.57) involves ordinary, not partial, differential equations, as would be the case if more than one state variable were involved. Having a single state variable in the problem is critical for further analytical development involving closed-loop (perfect) equilibria.

3 ANALYSIS OF A LANCHESTER DUOPOLY

Assume we have two competitors in a competition for market share, and that each wishes to maximize its discounted cash flow over an infinite horizon. We have for competitor 1

$$\max_{A_1} \int_0^\infty e^{-rt}(g_1 M - A_1)dt \qquad (3.1)$$

and for competitor 2

$$\max_{A_2} \int_0^\infty e^{-rt}[g_2(1 - M) - A_2]dt. \qquad (3.2)$$

The parameters g_1 and g_2 represent the economic values of market shares for competitors 1 and 2, respectively. Also, r is the discount rate, assumed equivalent for the two competitors.

Assume that M, the market share of competitor 1, varies across time according to a Lanchester model:

$$\dot{M} = \beta_1 A_1^{\alpha_1}(1 - M) - \beta_2 A_2^{\alpha_2}M. \qquad (3.3)$$

We wish to find Nash (noncooperative) equilibrium solutions for the advertising levels of the two competitors, A_1 and A_2, that vary across time. As discussed in chapter 2, we can pursue two kinds of Nash solutions, open-loop and closed-loop. The closed-loop equilibria that we will study

39

are those based on the perfect equilibrium concept of Case (1979). Accordingly, from this point we shall refer to perfect equilibria, $A_i(M)$, $i = 1, 2$, as *closed-loop* and those that vary with time specifically, $A_i(t)$, as *open-loop*. We shall study and compare both. Analytical derivations, particularly for closed-loop equilibria, will be done under steady-state conditions. Analytical investigation of the transient nature of closed-loop equilibria is very difficult, due to the multipicity and variety of such solutions, and investigation in this regard, for the model in this chapter as well as those in subsequent chapters, will be conducted numerically through specific examples.

Erickson (1985) has investigated properties of open-loop solutions of a duopoly Lanchester model, and we review the derivations in order to provide comparisons between open- and closed-loop solutions.

Open-Loop Solution

An open-loop solution to the problem (3.1)–(3.3) requires maximization of the current-value Hamiltonians

$$H_1 = g_1 M - A_1 + k_1[\beta_1 A_1^{\alpha_1}(1 - M) - \beta_2 A_2^{\alpha_2}M]$$
$$H_2 = g_2(1 - M) - A_2 + k_2[\beta_1 A_1^{\alpha_1}(1 - M) - \beta_2 A_2^{\alpha_2}M] \quad (3.4)$$

where the costate variables k_1, k_2 are subject to the following dynamic constraints:

$$\dot{k}_1 = rk_1 - \frac{\partial H_1}{\partial M} = (r + \beta_1 A_1^{\alpha_1} + \beta_2 A_2^{\alpha_2})k_1 - g_1$$

$$\dot{k}_2 = rk_2 - \frac{\partial H_2}{\partial M} = (r + \beta_1 A_1^{\alpha_1} + \beta_2 A_2^{\alpha_2})k_2 + g_2. \quad (3.5)$$

The costate variables k_1, k_2, have an economic interpretation, in that they represent the marginal values to competitors 1 and 2, respectively, of a change in market share M.

Setting $\partial H_1/\partial A_1 = 0$ and $\partial H_2/\partial A_2 = 0$ yields the following relationships:

$$k_1 = \frac{A_1^{1-\alpha_1}}{a_1\beta_1(1 - M)}$$
$$k_2 = \frac{-A_2^{1-\alpha_2}}{\alpha_2\beta_2 M}. \quad (3.6)$$

From the relationships in (3.6), we derive

$$\dot{k}_1 = \frac{A_1^{1-\alpha_1}}{\alpha_1\beta_1(1 - M)}\left(\frac{(1 - \alpha_1)\dot{A}_1}{A_1} + \beta_1 A_1^{\alpha_1} - \frac{\beta_2 A_2^{\alpha_2}M}{1 - M}\right)$$

$$\dot{k}_2 = \frac{-A_2^{1-\alpha_2}}{\alpha_2\beta_2 M}\left(\frac{(1 - \alpha_2)\dot{A}_2}{A_2} + \beta_2 A_2^{\alpha_2} - \frac{\beta_1 A_1^{\alpha_1}(1 - M)}{M}\right). \quad (3.7)$$

Substituting the relationships in (3.7) and (3.6) into constraints (3.5) yields the following dynamic relationships for the advertising variables, which are unencumbered by the costate variables:

$$\dot{A}_1 = \frac{A_1}{1 - \alpha_1}\left(r + \frac{\beta_2 A_2^{\alpha_2}}{1 - M} - \frac{g_1\alpha_1\beta_1(1 - M)}{A_1^{1-\alpha_1}}\right)$$

$$\dot{A}_2 = \frac{A_2}{1 - \alpha_2}\left(r + \frac{\beta_1 A_1^{\alpha_1}}{M} - \frac{g_2\alpha_2\beta_2 M}{A_2^{1-\alpha_2}}\right). \quad (3.8)$$

As Erickson (1985) shows, the relationships in (3.8) offer interesting insights regarding the temporal movement of open-loop advertising levels, at least for a zero discount rate r. In particular, a competitor's advertising rises across time while its rival's advertising declines only if the competitor's market share relative to its rival's is higher than its steady-state value and shrinking across time. Conversely, decreasing advertising coupled with increasing rival advertising requires relative market share to be lower than its steady-state value and rising. The dynamic use of advertising by the two competitors requires market shares that are not in steady state, in which case the competitors adjust advertising dynamically to allow shares to approach their steady-state levels.

Also of interest are results regarding advertising levels and market shares in steady state, that is, when $\dot{M} = \dot{A}_1 = \dot{A}_2 = 0$. Setting $\dot{M} = 0$ yields

$$\frac{M}{1 - M} = \frac{\beta_1 A_1^{\alpha_1}}{\beta_2 A_2^{\alpha_2}} \quad (3.9)$$

and

$$M = \frac{\beta_1 A_1^{\alpha_1}}{\beta_1 A_1^{\alpha_1} + \beta_2 A_2^{\alpha_2}}. \quad (3.10)$$

Setting $\dot{A}_1 = \dot{A}_2 = 0$ in equations (3.8) and exploiting the relationship in equation (3.10) yields the following equations (see appendix 3.1 for the proof):

$$\beta_2 A_2^{\alpha_2} = (\beta_1 A_1^{\alpha_1} + \beta_2 A_2^{\alpha_2})(\beta_1 A_1^{\alpha_1} + \beta_2 A_2^{\alpha_2} + r)\frac{A_1^{1-\alpha_1}}{g_1\alpha_1\beta_1}$$

$$\beta_1 A_1^{\alpha_1} = (\beta_1 A_1^{\alpha_1} + \beta_2 A_2^{\alpha_2})(\beta_1 A_1^{\alpha_1} + \beta_2 A_2^{\alpha_2} + r)\frac{A_2^{1-\alpha_2}}{g_2 \alpha_2 \beta_2} \qquad (3.11)$$

so that

$$\frac{M}{1-M} = \frac{\beta_1 A_1^{\alpha_1}}{\beta_2 A_2^{\alpha_2}} = \frac{g_1 \alpha_1 \beta_1 A_2^{1-\alpha_2}}{g_2 \alpha_2 \beta_2 A_1^{1-\alpha_1}}. \qquad (3.12)$$

The relationship (3.12) provides valuable insights regarding relative advertising levels and market shares in steady state. In particular, we have the following result:

$$\frac{A_1}{A_2} = \frac{g_1 \alpha_1}{g_2 \alpha_2}. \qquad (3.13)$$

That is, relative advertising in steady state depends directly on relative contribution g_1/g_2 as well as on the relative elasticity values α_1/α_2. Notice that relative advertising does not depend at all upon the advertising effectiveness parameters β_1, β_2. If the elasticities are equal ($\alpha_1 = \alpha_2 = \alpha$), then relative advertising depends *only on relative contribution*. Furthermore, under this latter condition of equal elasticities, relative market share in steady state shows the following relationship:

$$\frac{M}{1-M} = \frac{\beta_1}{\beta_2}\left(\frac{g_1}{g_2}\right)^{\alpha}. \qquad (3.14)$$

In steady state, relative market share depends on relative contribution, relative advertising effectiveness, and the value of the elasticity parameter α.

Closed-Loop Solution

To find a closed-loop solution to the Lanchester game (3.1)–(3.3), we use Case's concept of a perfect equilibrium (Case 1979). That is, we pursue advertising strategies $A_1(M)$, $A_2(M)$, such that each is optimal given the other competitor's strategy. Advertising levels are considered to be functions of the level of market share and to vary across time only in that market share varies. This is quite a different way to determine advertising levels, adjusting advertising as market share changes, than for open-loop strategies, in which advertising levels, although varying across time, are determined at the outset and are not subject to change over the duration of the game. As a consequence, we should not be surprised if closed-loop equilibrium strategies turn out to be quite different than open-loop strategies.

Consider the Hamiltonians (3.4), and identify *value functions* $V_1(M)$, $V_2(M)$ according to

$$V_1'(M) = k_1$$

$$V_2'(M) = k_2. \tag{3.15}$$

Maximizing the Hamiltonians with respect to advertising provides

$$\hat{A}_1(M, V_1', V_2') = [\alpha_1\beta_1 V_1'(1 - M)]^{1/(1-\alpha_1)} = A_1^*(M)$$

$$\hat{A}_2(M, V_1', V_2') = (-\alpha_2\beta_2 V_2'M)^{1/(1-\alpha_2)} = A_2^*(M). \tag{3.16}$$

Substituting the relationships in the system of equations (3.16) into the Hamiltonians (3.4), we arrive at the *Hamilton–Jacobi equations*:

$$g_1 M - [\alpha_1\beta_1 V_1'(1 - M)]^{1/(1-\alpha_1)}$$
$$+ V_1'\{\beta_1[\alpha_1\beta_1 V_1'(1 - M)]^{\alpha_1/(1-\alpha_1)}(1 - M) - \beta_2(-\alpha_2\beta_2 V_2'M)^{\alpha_2/(1-\alpha_2)}M\}$$
$$= rV_1 + c_1$$

$$g_2(1 - M) - (-\alpha_2\beta_2 V_2'M)^{1/(1-\alpha_2)}$$
$$+ V_2'\{\beta_1[\alpha_1\beta_1 V_1'(1 - M)]^{\alpha_1/(1-\alpha_1)}(1 - M) - \beta_2(-\alpha_2\beta_2 V_2'M)^{\alpha_2/(1-\alpha_2)}M\}$$
$$= rV_2 + c_2 \tag{3.17}$$

where c_1, c_2 are arbitrary constants. Closed-loop equilibrium strategies could be obtained by solving equations (3.17) for $V_1(M)$, $V_2(M)$ and applying equations (3.16). Instead, however, we will examine an equivalent system of equations not involving the value functions. Solving equations (3.16) for V_1', V_2' (and dropping the asterisks on the advertising functions),

$$V_1'(M) = \frac{A_1^{1-\alpha_1}(M)}{\alpha_1\beta_1(1 - M)}$$

$$V_2'(M) = \frac{-A_2^{1-\alpha_2}(M)}{\alpha_2\beta_2 M}. \tag{3.18}$$

Also,

$$V_1(M) = \int^M \frac{A_1^{1-\alpha_1}(m)}{\alpha_1\beta_1(1 - m)}\,dm$$

$$V_2(M) = -\int^M \frac{A_2^{1-\alpha_2}(m)}{\alpha_2\beta_2 m}\,dm \tag{3.19}$$

where the lower limits on the integrals in equations (3.19) are fixed but arbitrary. Substituting equations (3.19) and (3.18) into equations (3.17) provides the following system of equations:

$$g_1 M - A_1 + \frac{A_1^{1-\alpha_1}}{\alpha_1 \beta_1 (1 - M)} [\beta_1 A_1^{\alpha_1}(1 - M) - \beta_2 A_2^{\alpha_2} M]$$

$$= r \int^M \frac{A_1^{1-\alpha_1}(m)}{\alpha_1 \beta_1 (1 - m)} dm + c_1$$

$$g_2 (1 - M) - A_2 - \frac{A_2^{1-\alpha_2}}{\alpha_2 \beta_2 M} [\beta_1 A_1^{\alpha_1}(1 - M) - \beta_2 A_2^{\alpha_2} M]$$

$$= -r \int^M \frac{A_2^{1-\alpha_2}(m)}{\alpha_2 \beta_2 m} dm + c_2. \tag{3.20}$$

The equations in (3.20) are differentiable in terms of M, and lead directly to the following system:

$$\frac{1 - \alpha_1}{A_1} [\beta_1 A_1^{\alpha_1}(1 - M) - \beta_2 A_2^{\alpha_2} M] A_1' - \frac{\alpha_2 \beta_2}{A_2^{1-\alpha_2}} M A_2'$$

$$= r - g_1 \frac{\alpha_1 \beta_1}{A_1^{1-\alpha_1}} (1 - M) + \frac{\beta_2 A_2^{\alpha_2}}{1 - M}$$

$$\frac{1 - \alpha_2}{A_2} [\beta_1 A_1^{\alpha_1}(1 - M) - \beta_2 A_2^{\alpha_2} M] A_2' + \frac{\alpha_1 \beta_1}{A_1^{1-\alpha_1}} (1 - M) A_1'$$

$$= r - g_2 \frac{\alpha_2 \beta_2}{A_2^{1-\alpha_2}} M + \frac{\beta_1 A_1^{\alpha_1}}{M}. \tag{3.21}$$

Making the following identities

$$B = \frac{1 - \alpha_1}{A_1} \frac{1 - \alpha_2}{A_2} \dot{M}^2 + \frac{\alpha_1 \beta_1}{A_1^{1-\alpha_1}} \frac{\alpha_2 \beta_2}{A_2^{1-\alpha_2}} M(1 - M)$$

$$C = r - g_1 \frac{\alpha_1 \beta_1}{A_1^{1-\alpha_1}} (1 - M) + \frac{\beta_2 A_2^{\alpha_2}}{1 - M}$$

$$D = r - g_2 \frac{\alpha_2 \beta_2}{A_2^{1-\alpha_2}} M + \frac{\beta_1 A_1^{\alpha_1}}{M} \tag{3.22}$$

the system can be expressed in the following standard form (see appendix 3.2):

$$A_1' = B^{-1} \left(\frac{1 - \alpha_2}{A_2} \dot{M} C + \frac{\alpha_2 \beta_2}{A_2^{1-\alpha_2}} M D \right)$$

$$A_2' = B^{-1} \left(\frac{1 - \alpha_1}{A_1} \dot{M} D - \frac{\alpha_1 \beta_1}{A_1^{1-\alpha_1}} (1 - M) C \right) \tag{3.23}$$

where, of course, $\dot{M}$ is defined by the dynamic constraint (3.3). For given boundary conditions, the system (3.23) can be solved with numerical methods.

Additional insights can be obtained by setting the discount rate r to zero. In this case, we have the following relationships involving competitors' advertising and market share:

$$g_1 M - A_1 + \frac{A_1^{1-\alpha_1}}{\alpha_1 \beta_1 (1 - M)} [\beta_1 A_1^{\alpha_1}(1 - M) - \beta_2 A_2^{\alpha_2} M] = c_1$$

$$g_2(1 - M) - A_2 - \frac{A_2^{1-\alpha_2}}{\alpha_2 \beta_2 M} [\beta_1 A_1^{\alpha_1}(1 - M) - \beta_2 A_2^{\alpha_2} M] = c_2. \quad (3.24)$$

One particular aspect of the relationships in (3.24) to note is that the solutions depend on the (arbitrary) constants c_1 and c_2. *Any* solution to the equations in (3.24), for any pair (c_1, c_2), is a closed-loop solution. There is, in general, an abundance of closed-loop solutions. As an example will show, the functional relationships between market share and the advertising of the competitors can take a variety of shapes, which makes it difficult to derive general results, at least in terms of temporal patterns.

Let us focus on steady-state aspects of the solutions. Steady state, for closed-loop solutions as defined, means that $\dot{M} = 0$, and therefore that $\dot{A}_1 = \dot{A}_2 = 0$. The system (3.24) can be expressed as follows:

$$g_1 M - A_1 + \frac{A_1^{1-\alpha_1}}{\alpha_1 \beta_1 (1 - M)} \dot{M} = c_1$$

$$g_2(1 - M) - A_2 - \frac{A_2^{1-\alpha_2}}{\alpha_2 \beta_2 M} \dot{M} = c_2. \quad (3.25)$$

At steady state, accordingly, we have the following relationships:

$$g_1 M - A_1 = c_1$$

$$g_2(1 - M) - A_2 = c_2. \quad (3.26)$$

As the relationships in (3.26) show, the constants c_1 and c_2 equal the steady-state profit rates of competitors 1 and 2, respectively. A reasonable way to limit the constants, as a consequence, is to require that they be within the range of potential nonnegative profit rates, i.e., $0 \leq c_1 \leq g_1$, $0 \leq c_2 \leq g_2$. Values of c_1 and c_2 outside those limits would suggest either unattainable or undesirably negative profits in steady state, and as such do not represent particularly realistic games.

It is also clear from equations (3.26) that, in steady state,

$$A_1 = g_1 M - c_1$$

$$A_2 = g_2(1 - M) - c_2. \tag{3.27}$$

Furthermore, steady state implies, from equation (3.3), that

$$\frac{M}{1 - M} = \frac{\beta_1 A_1^{\alpha_1}}{\beta_2 A_2^{\alpha_2}} \tag{3.28}$$

and therefore that

$$\frac{M}{1 - M} = \frac{\beta_1(g_1 M - c_1)^{\alpha_1}}{\beta_2[g_2(1 - M) - c_2]^{\alpha_2}}. \tag{3.29}$$

Equation (3.29) defines M implicitly as a function of the various parameters of the problem, and can be used to investigate the effects of the parameters on market share in steady state. It should be recognized that, in general, there may be multiple values of M that satisfy equation (3.29). That is, there may be multiple steady states.

Taking partial derivatives in equation (3.29) and rearranging terms produces the following relationships between market share M and the parameters of the model:

$$\frac{\partial M}{\partial \alpha_1} = G^{-1} M(1 - M) \ln(g_1 M - c_1)$$

$$\frac{\partial M}{\partial \alpha_2} = -G^{-1} M(1 - M) \ln[g_2(1 - M) - c_2]$$

$$\frac{\partial M}{\partial \beta_1} = \frac{G^{-1} M(1 - M)}{\beta_1}$$

$$\frac{\partial M}{\partial \beta_2} = \frac{-G^{-1} M(1 - M)}{\beta_2}$$

$$\frac{\partial M}{\partial g_1} = \frac{G^{-1} \alpha_1 M^2(1 - M)}{(g_1 M - c_1)}$$

$$\frac{\partial M}{\partial g_2} = \frac{-G^{-1} \alpha_2 M(1 - M)^2}{g_2(1 - M) - c_2} \tag{3.30}$$

where

$$G = 1 - \frac{g_1 \alpha_1 M(1 - M)}{g_1 M - c_1} - \frac{g_2 \alpha_2 M(1 - M)}{g_2(1 - M) - c_2}.$$

The value of G may be either positive or negative, depending on the value of market share M. For the "reasonable" values of c_1, c_2 indicated above, we have the following lemma regarding G as a function of M:

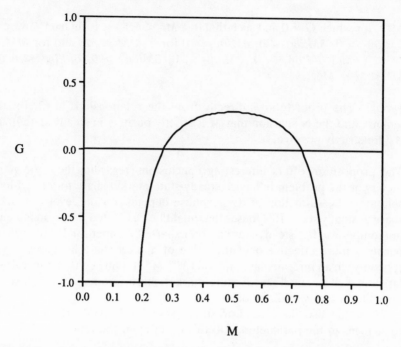

Figure 3.1.   *G* as a Function of *M*.

Lemma.   Assume $0 \leq c_1 \leq g_1$, $0 \leq c_2 \leq g_2$. Also, assume that advertising levels A_1, A_2 are strictly positive at steady state. Then, in the interval $0 \leq M \leq 1$, there are at most two values of M, call them M^*, M^{**}, at which G changes sign. Furthermore, if $0 < M^* < M^{**} < 1$, then $G < 0$ for $0 < M < M^*$, $G > 0$ for $M^* < M < M^{**}$, and $G < 0$ for $M^{**} < M < 1$.

Proof.   See appendix 3.3.

The relationship between G and steady-state market share M is illustrated in figure 3.1.

The responsiveness of the steady-state market share to parameters of the problem depends on its level at steady state. The response to changes in the elasticities α_1, α_2 cannot be determined unequivocally, but we have the following proposition for the remaining parameters:

Proposition 3.1.   Assume that $0 \leq c_1 \leq g_1$, $0 \leq c_2 \leq g_2$, and that advertising A_1, A_2, is strictly positive in steady state. If there exist M^*,

M^{**}, for which $G = 0$ and such that $0 < M^* < M^{**} < 1$, then $\partial M/\partial \beta_1 < 0$, $\partial M/\partial \beta_2 > 0$, $\partial M/\partial g_1 < 0$, $\partial M/\partial g_2 > 0$ for $0 < M < M^*$ and for $M^{**} < M < 1$, and $\partial M/\partial \beta_1 > 0$, $\partial M/\partial \beta_2 < 0$, $\partial M/\partial g_1 > 0$, $\partial M/\partial g_2 < 0$ for $M^* < M < M^{**}$.

Proof. The proof follows directly from the relationships in (3.30), the lemma, and the conclusion that M is strictly positive in steady state if A_1, A_2 are strictly positive.

The proposition offers interesting conclusions regarding how the parameters of the problem influence steady-state market share for closed-loop solutions. The direction of the response depends on the level of market share at steady state. Responses that might be "expected," i.e., an increase in (competitor 1's) steady-state market share if competitor 1's advertising becomes more effective or if the value of market share increases, occur (possibly) in an intermediate interval (M^*, M^{**}). Outside that interval, for large as well as small steady-state market share, the response is just the opposite in terms of direction.

We would also like to see how steady-state levels of advertising respond to changes in the parameters. Do this in terms of the ratio

$$AR = \frac{A_1}{A_2} = \frac{g_1 M - c_1}{g_2(1 - M) - c_2}. \tag{3.31}$$

For strictly positive A_1, A_2, we have that

$$\frac{\partial AR}{\partial M} = \frac{g_1[g_2(1 - M) - c_2] + g_2(g_1 M - c_1)}{[g_2(1 - M) - c_2]^2} > 0. \tag{3.32}$$

We break the advertising results into two propositions. The first involves the responsiveness of the steady-state advertising ratio to the advertising effectiveness parameters β_1, β_2:

Proposition 3.2. Assume $0 \leq c_1 \leq g_1$, $0 \leq c_2 \leq g_2$, and A_1, A_2 strictly positive in steady state. Then $\partial AR/\partial \beta_1$, $\partial AR/\partial \beta_2$, are of the same sign as $\partial M/\partial \beta_1$, $\partial M/\partial \beta_2$, respectively, and AR follows the same pattern as that for M described in proposition 3.1.

Proof. The proof follows from equation (3.32) and $\partial AR/\partial \beta_i = (\partial AR/\partial M)(\partial M/\partial \beta_i)$ for $i = 1, 2$.

The response of the steady-state advertising ratio is in the same direction as that for market share, and therefore follows the same pattern as indicated in proposition 3.1. The advertising ratio increases for an increase in competitor 1's advertising effectiveness, and decreases for an increase in competitor 2's effectiveness, but only for an intermediate interval of M. For large or small M, the direction of the response is reversed.

The results regarding the response to changes in g_1, g_2—the values of market share to competitors 1, 2, respectively—requires the equality of the two elasticity parameters, $\alpha_1 = \alpha_2$:

Proposition 3.3. Assume $0 \leqslant c_1 \leqslant g_1$, $0 \leqslant c_2 \leqslant g_2$, and A_1, A_2 strictly positive in steady state. Further, assume that $\alpha_1 = \alpha_2$. Then $\partial AR/\partial g_1$, $\partial AR/\partial g_2$, are of the same sign as $\partial M/\partial g_1$, $\partial M/\partial g_2$, respectively, and AR follows the same pattern as that for M described in proposition 3.1.

Proof. See appendix 3.4.

If we can assume that $\alpha_1 = \alpha_2$, we have the same pattern for the steady-state advertising ratio, as it responds to changes in g_1 and g_2, as that for steady-state market share. In an intermediate interval for M, the advertising ratio responds positively to an increase in g_1 and negatively to an increase in g_2. For extreme values of M, the direction of the response is reversed.

Example

A specific example is useful for illustrating dynamics of a solution, and for comparing closed-loop with open-loop solutions. Assume a symmetric situation involving the two competitors, with the following parameter values:

$$\alpha_1 = \alpha_2 = .5$$
$$\beta_1 = \beta_2 = .5$$
$$g_1 = g_2 = 1$$
$$c_1 = c_2 = c$$
$$r = 0. \tag{3.33}$$

We will continue to assume a zero discount rate. Also, since closed-loop solutions can vary dramatically with $c = c_1 = c_2$, we will let that parameter take on a variety of values.

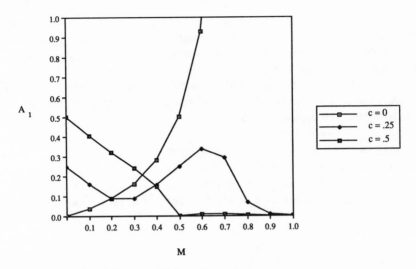

Figure 3.2.   Closed-Loop Equilibrium Strategies.

With the parameter values in (3.33), the closed-loop solution can be expressed in closed form:

$$A_1 =$$

$$\frac{2(1-M-c)M^2/(1-M)^2 - (M-c) + 2\sqrt{(M-c)^2 - (M-c)(1-M-c)M^2/(1-M)^2 + (1-M-c)^2M^4/(1-M)^4}}{3}$$

$$A_2 =$$

$$\frac{2(M-c)(1-M)^2/M^2 - (1-M-c) + 2\sqrt{(1-M-c)^2 - (1-M-c)(M-c)(1-M)^2/M^2 + (M-c)^2(1-M)^4/M^4}}{3}.$$

$$(3.34)$$

With the symmetry in the example, we have that $A_1(M) = A_2(1 - M)$.

Figure 3.2 shows the closed-loop solution for the example, for three different values of c. The solution for $c = 0$ is particularly dissatisfying, in that it indicates advertising at low rates when market share is low (when advertising is needed to attract market share), and at high (approaching infinite) rates when market share is high. The $c = .25$ solution shows similar tendencies, low advertising at low market shares and high advertising at high shares, although the curve is not monotonic, and shows relatively high advertising at $M = 0$ and zero advertising at $M = 1$.

The solution for $c = .5$ is of particular interest, since for that value, the (equal) steady-state profits of the two competitors are at their maximum. Notice that $A_1 (= A_2) = 0$ for $M = .5$, which, as it turns out, is the unique steady-state market share. (There is more on steady state below.) There are two distinct portions of the $c = .5$ solution curve. In the interval $M = [0, .5]$, A_1 falls from a value of .5 to zero. For M larger than .5, the curve rises slightly before declining toward zero. What the solution for $c = .5$ basically indicates is that, if a competitor's market share is low (less than .5), advertising should be at a high level, to attract share from its rival. Advertising then decreases toward zero as the market share approaches a value of .5. The two competitors maximize their long-run profits by not advertising, and not taking share from each other, once they achieve equal market shares.

Steady-state analysis of market shares provides interesting results. For this symmetric problem, $M = .5$ is always a steady-state market share, but for certain values of c, that value is not the only steady-state market share. Appendix 3.5 shows that, for $c < .25$, there are three distinct market share levels that may exist in steady state:

$$M_1 = .5 + \sqrt{.25 - c}$$
$$M_2 = .5 + \sqrt{.25 - c}$$
$$M_3 = .5 \tag{3.35}$$

For values of c equal to and exceeding .25, $M = .5$ is the only steady-state value.

The dynamics of market share and advertising as they approach steady state can be determined numerically, by using the formulas in (3.34) to provide A_1 and A_2 for a current value of M, and updating M by

$$\Delta M = \frac{\sqrt{A_1}(1 - M) - \sqrt{A_2}M}{2}. \tag{3.36}$$

Period-by-period advertising and market shares are calculated in this way until successive market shares are sufficiently close together.

Figure 3.3 shows the time paths of the closed-loop advertising strategies and market share for three levels of c, all of which are less than .25. Beginning market share in all cases is .25. Competitor 2's advertising, A_2, is not shown for $c = 0$, since it starts at 2.57 in the initial period and grows from there toward an infinite level. Notice how market share for each value

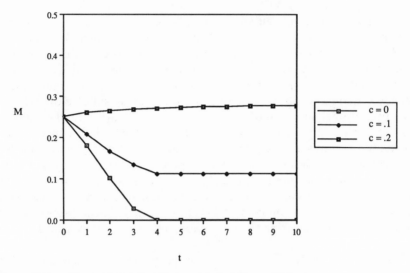

Figure 3.3a.   Closed-Loop Equilibrium Market-Share Paths.

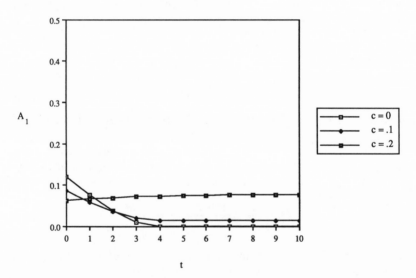

Figure 3.3b.   Closed-Loop Equilibrium Advertising Paths for Competitor 1.

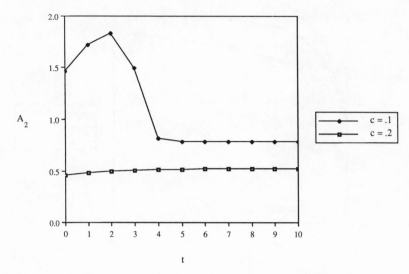

Figure 3.3c.   Closed-Loop Equilibrium Advertising Paths for Competitor 2.

of c tends toward a unique value that is not equal to .5. In fact, numerical analysis for a number of different starting values for M show that market share will tend toward either $.5 + \sqrt{25 - c}$ or $.5 - \sqrt{25 - c}$, depending upon whether the initial value is greater or lesser, respectively, than .5. For $c < .25$, market share will achieve a value of .5 only if it starts at that value.

Figure 3.4 shows the dynamics of the advertising strategies and market share for values of c larger than .25. For each c, market share tends toward the only possible steady-state value of .5. As such, given the symmetric nature of the example, it would not be unreasonable to restrict c to be greater than .25 and to concentrate on the dynamic patterns observed in figure 3.4. The advertising patterns therein indicate that monotonic change across time is a frequent occurrence but does not always hold. In particular, for $c = .3$, the advertising for competitor 2 grows before starting to decline slowly. Also, competing advertising can proceed in either the same or opposite directions. For $c = .4$, advertising grows across time for competitor 2 while declining for competitor 1. For $c = .5$, which yields the largest steady-state profits for the competitors, the advertising for both declines to zero as competitor 1's market share approaches .5.

For the purpose of comparison, the (single) open-loop solution to the problem in this example is shown in figure 3.5. Details for obtaining the open-loop solution, including the algorithm used, are in appendix 3.6.

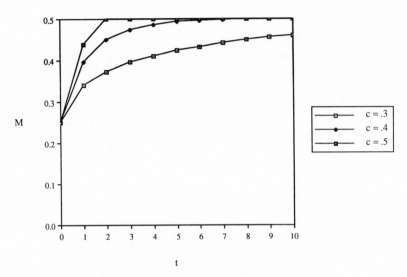

Figure 3.4a.   Closed-Loop Equilibrium Market-Share Paths.

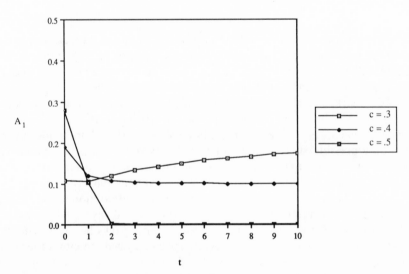

Figure 3.4b.   Closed-Loop Equilibrium Advertising Paths for Competitor 1.

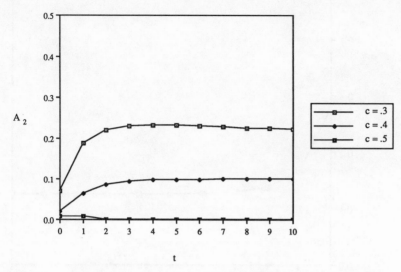

Figure 3.4c.   Closed-Loop Equilibrium Advertising Paths for Competitor 2.

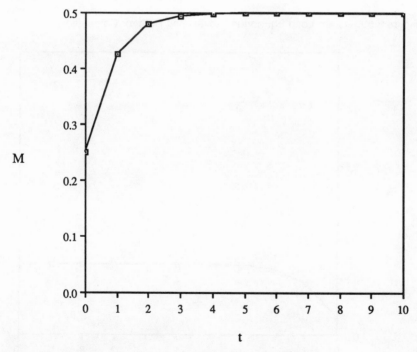

Figure 3.5a.   Open-Loop Equilibrium Market-Share Path.

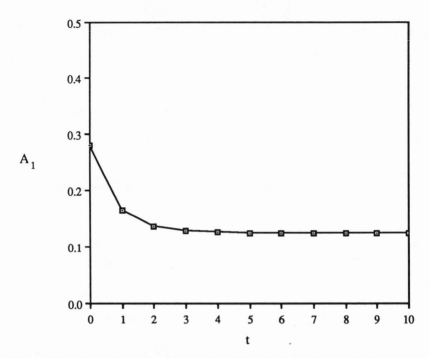

Figure 3.5b. Open-Loop Equilibrium Advertising Path for Competitor 1.

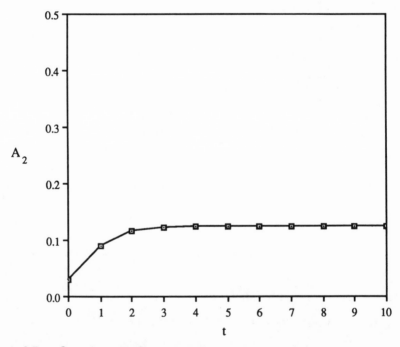

Figure 3.5c. Open-Loop Equilibrium Advertising Path for Competitor 2.

Market share, assumed to be .25 initially, converges to its steady-state value of .5. Advertising is initially heavier for competitor 1 than for competitor 2, which allows market share to increase in the initial periods. Thereafter, advertising levels for the two competitors proceed in opposite directions—declining for competitor 1 and growing for competitor 2—and approach equal steady-state values. This general dynamic pattern holds for all initial market-share values that are less than .5. For initial market shares exceeding .5, the pattern is reversed for the two competitors.

In terms of advertising dynamics, the solution for $c = .4$ is the closed-loop solution closest, of those shown, to the open-loop solution. For this closed-loop solution, as for the open-loop solution, competitor advertising levels move in opposite directions in the approach to steady state. Interestingly, the ($c = .4$) closed-loop solution provides higher steady-state profits for the competitors than does the open-loop solution. Indeed, all closed-loop solutions with c exceeding .375 produce higher steady-state profits than does the open-loop solution. The conclusion that profits can be higher with certain closed-loop equilibria should not be a surprise, since there is an abundance of closed-loop solutions from which to choose.

Comparison of Closed-Loop and Open-Loop Solutions

Given the different ways that closed-loop and open-loop solutions are formed—open-loop strategies are formulated as functions of time but cannot be changed over the planning horizon, while closed-loop strategies are permitted to respond to the current state of the market—it is not surprising that there are differences between the two. The primary basic difference is that there are a much larger number of closed-loop solutions. That is to be expected, perhaps, given the flexible nature of closed-loop strategies as the state of the market changes, versus the fixed nature of open-loop strategies. At the same time, as the example shows, it may be possible to find closed-loop strategies that are similar to open-loop strategies. The example also indicates that closed-loop solutions can likely be found that provide more long-run profits to the competitors than do open-loop solutions.

There are also basic differences between open-loop and closed-loop solutions in the way they respond to changes in the parameters of the problem. If we have equal advertising elasticities $\alpha_1 = \alpha_2$, analysis of open-loop solutions in steady state show that relative market share (competitor 1's steady-state share divided by competitor 2's) responds positively to an increase in the advertising-effectiveness parameter for competitor 1, β_1, and to an increase in the value of market share to 1, g_1, and responds negatively to an increase in β_2 or g_2. For closed-loop solutions, the response of market share is more equivocal. The direction of the response depends on the level of steady-state market share, of which there may be multiple values. Only for an intermediate region of market share is the response in the same direction as that for open-loop solutions, should such a region exist at all.

Comparison of the effects of parameter changes on steady-state advertising shows even more dramatic differences. Relative advertising (competitor 1 to competitor 2) in steady state for open-loop solutions is not dependent on the effectiveness parameters β_1, β_2. For closed-loop solutions, however, the story is different. Closed-loop advertising strategies depend directly upon market share, and since market share in steady state is affected by β_1 and β_2, so too is advertising. Furthermore, the direction of the response depends on the level of steady-state market share. Finally, closed-loop relative advertising may respond to the market-share value parameters g_1, g_2, in the same direction as open-loop advertising, but only for intermediate levels of steady-state market share.

In summary, in this chapter we have examined both open-loop and closed-loop advertising strategies for a Lanchester duopoly. Through theoretical analysis of the solutions in steady state and study of a specific example, we have found that the two types of approaches generate solutions that are quite different in nature. Perhaps the most dramatic difference is that closed-loop advertising strategies in steady state are influenced by the effectiveness of advertising, while open-loop strategies are not.

Appendix 3.1.   Proof of relationship (3.11)

Setting $A_1 = 0$ yields

$$g_1 \frac{\alpha_1 \beta_1}{A_1^{1-\alpha_1}} (1 - M) = \frac{\beta_2 A_2^{\alpha_2}}{1 - M} + r$$

$$g_1 \frac{\alpha_1 \beta_1}{A_1^{1-\alpha_1}} (1 - M)^2 = \beta_2 A_2^{\alpha_2} + r(1 - M) \tag{A3.1}$$

Exploiting equations (3.8),

$$\frac{g_1 (\alpha_1 \beta_1 / A_1^{1-\alpha_1})(\beta_2 A_2^{\alpha_2})^2}{(\beta_1 A_1^{\alpha_1} + \beta_2 A_2^{\alpha_2})^2} = \beta_2 A_2^{\alpha_2} + \frac{r \beta_2 A_2^{\alpha_2}}{\beta_1 A_1^{\alpha_1} + \beta_2 A_2^{\alpha_2}}$$

$$\frac{g_1(\alpha_1\beta_1/A_1^{1-\alpha_1})(\beta_2 A_2^{\alpha_2})}{(\beta_1 A_1^{\alpha_1} + \beta_2 A_2^{\alpha_2})^2} = 1 + \frac{r}{\beta_1 A_1^{\alpha_1} + \beta_2 A_2^{\alpha_2}} \tag{A3.2}$$

so that

$$\beta_2 A_2^{\alpha_2} = [(\beta_1 A_1^{\alpha_1} + \beta_2 A_2^{\alpha_2})^2 + r(\beta_1 A_1^{\alpha_1} + \beta_2 A_2^{\alpha_2})] \frac{A_1^{1-\alpha_1}}{g_1 \alpha_1 \beta_1}$$

$$= (\beta_1 A_1^{\alpha_1} + \beta_2 A_2^{\alpha_2})(\beta_1 A_1^{\alpha_1} + \beta_2 A_2^{\alpha_2} + r) \frac{A_1^{1-\alpha_1}}{g_1 \alpha_1 \beta_1}. \tag{A3.3}$$

Identically, setting $\dot{A}_2 = 0$ yields the second equation in (3.11).

Appendix 3.2. Proof of relationship (3.23)

Define B, C, D, as in the equations in (3.22). Then, from the equations in (3.21),

$$\frac{1 - \alpha_1}{A_1} \dot{M} A_1' - \frac{\alpha_2 \beta_2}{A_2^{1-\alpha_2}} M A_2' = C$$

$$\frac{1 - \alpha_2}{A_2} \dot{M} A_2' - \frac{\alpha_1 \beta_1}{A_1^{1-\alpha_1}} (1 - M) A_1' = D \tag{A3.4}$$

or, in matrix form,

$$E \begin{bmatrix} A_1' \\ A_2' \end{bmatrix} = \begin{bmatrix} C \\ D \end{bmatrix} \tag{A3.5}$$

where

$$E = \begin{bmatrix} \dfrac{1 - \alpha_1}{A_1} \dot{M} & -\dfrac{\alpha_2 \beta_2}{A_2^{1-\alpha_2}} M \\ \dfrac{\alpha_1 \beta_1}{A_1^{1-\alpha_1}} (1 - M) & \dfrac{1 - \alpha_2}{A_2} \dot{M} \end{bmatrix} \tag{A3.6}$$

so that

$$\begin{bmatrix} A_1' \\ A_2' \end{bmatrix} = E^{-1} \begin{bmatrix} C \\ D \end{bmatrix} \tag{A3.7}$$

and

$$
\begin{aligned}
E^{-1} &= \left(\frac{1-\alpha_1}{A_1} \frac{1-\alpha_2}{A_2} \dot{M}^2 + \frac{\alpha_1 \beta_1}{A_1^{1-\alpha_1}} \frac{\alpha_2 \beta_2}{A_2^{1-\alpha_2}} M(1-M) \right)^{-1} \\
&\qquad \cdot \begin{bmatrix} \dfrac{1-\alpha_2}{A_2}\dot{M} & \dfrac{\alpha_2 \beta_2}{A_2^{1-\alpha_2}} M \\[2ex] -\dfrac{\alpha_1 \beta_1}{A_1^{1-\alpha_1}}(1-M) & \dfrac{1-\alpha_1}{A_1}\dot{M} \end{bmatrix} \\
&= B^{-1} \begin{bmatrix} \dfrac{1-\alpha_2}{A_2}\dot{M} & \dfrac{\alpha_2 \beta_2}{A_2^{1-\alpha_2}} M \\[2ex] -\dfrac{\alpha_1 \beta_1}{A_1^{1-\alpha_1}}(1-M) & \dfrac{1-\alpha_1}{A_1}\dot{M} \end{bmatrix}.
\end{aligned}
\tag{A3.8}
$$

Appendix 3.3. Proof of lemma

Let G be as defined. Then

$$
G = \frac{f(M)}{(g_1 M - c_1)[g_2(1-M) - c_2]}
\tag{A3.9}
$$

where the denominator is strictly positive by assumption ($A_1 = g_1 M - c_1$ and $A_2 = g_2(1-M) - c_2$ at steady state), and

$$
\begin{aligned}
f(M) &= (g_1 M - c_1)[g_2(1-M) - c_2] \\
&\quad - [g_2(1-M) - c_2]g_1 \alpha_1 M(1-M) - (g_1 M - c_1)g_2 \alpha_2 M(1-M) \\
&= g_1 g_2(\alpha_2 - \alpha_1)M^3 - [g_1 g_2(1 + a_2 - 2\alpha_1) + c_1 g_2 \alpha_2 + c_2 g_1 \alpha_1]M^2 \\
&\quad + [g_1 g_2(1 - \alpha_1) + c_1 g_2(1 + \alpha_2) - c_2 g_1(1 - \alpha_1)]M - c_1(g_2 - c_2).
\end{aligned}
\tag{A3.10}
$$

The proof follows from the fact that $f(M)$ is a cubic and from its behavior in the interval $[0, 1]$ of M. Now,

$$
f(0) = -c_1(g_2 - c_2) \le 0
\tag{A3.11}
$$

and

$$
f(1) = -c_2(g_1 - c_1) \le 0.
\tag{A3.12}
$$

Also,

$$
f'(0) = [g_1(g_2 - c_2)(1 - \alpha_1) + c_1 g_2(1 + \alpha_2)] \ge 0
\tag{A3.13}
$$

and

$$f'(1) = -[g_2(g_1 - c_1)(1 - \alpha_2) + c_2g_1(1 + \alpha_1)] \leq 0. \quad (A3.14)$$

In the interval $0 \leq M \leq 1$, $f(M)$ starts out (at $M = 0$) being nonpositive, and finishes (at $M = 1$) being nonpositive. Since $f(M)$ is a cubic equation, it may become zero at (at most) three points. However, since $f(M)$ is nondecreasing at $M = 0$ and nonincreasing at $M = 1$, it can equal zero only twice, at the most, as M ranges from 0 to 1. Therefore, if $f(M)$ becomes positive at all, it is between M^* and M^{**}, the two points in the interval $[0, 1]$ for which $f(M) = 0$.

Appendix 3.4. Proof of proposition 3.3

Taking the partial derivative of AR with respect to g_1 and rearranging terms yields

$$\frac{\partial AR}{\partial g_1} = G^{-1}M[g_2(1 - M) - c_2]^{-2}[g_2(1 - M) - c_2 \\ + g_2M(1 - M)(\alpha_1 - \alpha_2)] \quad (A3.15)$$

where G is defined in equations (3.30) and is the foundation, through the lemma, for the results in proposition 3.1. Also

$$\frac{\partial AR}{\partial g_2} = -G^{-1}(1 - M)[g_2(1 - M) - c_2]^{-2}[g_1M - c_1 \\ + g_1M(1 - M)(\alpha_2 - \alpha_1)]. \quad (A3.16)$$

If $\alpha_1 = \alpha_2$, $\partial AR/\partial g_1$ is of the same sign, and $\partial AR/\partial g_2$ is of the opposite sign, as G. The proposition follows.

Appendix 3.5. Steady-state analysis for the example

At steady state, we have the following relationship involving market share M:

$$\frac{M}{1 - M} = \sqrt{\frac{M - c}{1 - M - c}}. \quad (A3.17)$$

The squaring of both sides and algebraic manipulation provides the following cubic equation in M:

$$M^3 - \frac{3}{2}M^2 + \left(c + \frac{1}{2}\right)M - \frac{c}{2} = 0. \tag{A3.18}$$

The roots of this equation are obtained by calculating

$$Q = \frac{3(c + 1/2) - (-3/2)^2}{9} = \frac{4c - 1}{12}$$

$$R = \frac{9(-3/2)(c + 1/2) - 27(-c/2) - 2(-3/2)^3}{54} = 0 \tag{A3.19}$$

and the discriminant

$$Q^3 + R^2 = \frac{(4c - 1)^3}{1728}. \tag{A3.20}$$

For $c < 1/4$, the discriminant is negative, and all three roots are real:

$$M_1 = 2\sqrt{-\frac{4c - 1}{12}} \cos \frac{\pi}{6} - \frac{-3/2}{3} = \sqrt{\frac{1}{4} - c} + \frac{1}{2}$$

$$M_2 = 2\sqrt{-\frac{4c - 1}{12}} \cos \frac{5\pi}{6} - \frac{-3/2}{3} = \sqrt{\frac{1}{4} - c} + \frac{1}{2}$$

$$M_3 = 2\sqrt{-\frac{4c - 1}{12}} \cos \frac{3\pi}{2} - \frac{-3/2}{3} = \frac{1}{2}. \tag{A3.21}$$

For $c = 1/4$, all three roots are equal:

$$M_1 = M_2 = M_3 = \frac{1}{2}. \tag{A3.22}$$

For $c > 1/4$, the discriminant is positive, and only one root is real:

$$M = (R + \sqrt{Q^3 + R^2})^{1/3} + (R - \sqrt{Q^3 + R^2})^{1/3} - \frac{-3/2}{3} = \frac{1}{2}. \tag{A3.23}$$

Appendix 3.6. Open-loop solution algorithm for the example

We have the following Hamiltonians for the problem in the example:

$$H_1 = g_1 M - A_1 + k_1 \dot{M}$$

$$H_2 = g_2(1 - M) - A_2 + k_2 \dot{M} \tag{A3.24}$$

where

$$\dot{M} = .5[\sqrt{A_1}(1 - M) - \sqrt{A_2} M] \tag{A3.25}$$

and

$$\dot{k}_1 = .5(\sqrt{A_1} + \sqrt{A_2})k_1 - 1$$
$$\dot{k}_2 = .5(\sqrt{A_1} + \sqrt{A_2})k_2 + 1. \qquad (A3.26)$$

Setting $\partial H_1 = 0$ and $\partial H_2 = 0$ yields the following relationships for advertising, given values for market share M and costate variables k_1, k_2:

$$A_1 = \left[(1 - M)\frac{k_1}{4}\right]^2$$

$$A_2 = \left(\frac{-Mk_2}{4}\right)^2. \qquad (A3.27)$$

It is assumed that the solution approaches a steady state. This yields the following terminal conditions for the costate variables:

$$k_1 = 2\sqrt{2}$$
$$k_2 = -2\sqrt{2}. \qquad (A3.28)$$

The following algorithm is used to solve the problem numerically:

1. Set the initial value $M(0)$. Also, set terminal values $k_1(T)$, $k_2(T)$ as in equations (A3.28).
2. Choose beginning values $A_1(t)$, $A_2(t)$ for $t = 1, 2, \ldots, T$.
3. For $t = 1, 2, \ldots, T$, determine $M(t)$ through forward integration, using equation (A3.25).
4. For $t = T - 1, T - 2, \ldots, 0$, determine $k_1(t)$, $k_2(t)$ through backward integration, using equations (A3.26).
5. For $t = 1, 2, \ldots, T$, determine $A_1(t)$, $A_2(t)$ through equations (A3.27). If, for each $t = 1, 2, \ldots, T$, $A_1(t)$ and $A_2(t)$ are sufficiently close to the corresponding values for the previous iteration, stop. Otherwise, return to step 3.

4 ANALYSIS OF A VIDALE–WOLFE DUOPOLY

In this chapter, we analyze the Vidale–Wolfe model introduced in chapter 2. In this model, it is assumed that the two competitors have the following maximization problems:

$$\max_{A_1} \int_0^\infty e^{-rt}\left(h_1 \frac{\gamma_1}{\gamma_1 + \gamma_2} S - A_1\right) dt$$

$$\max_{A_2} \int_0^\infty e^{-rt}\left(h_2 \frac{\gamma_2}{\gamma_1 + \gamma_2} S - A_2\right) dt \tag{4.1}$$

which are subject to the dynamic constraint

$$\dot{S} = (\beta_1 A_1^{\alpha_1} + \beta_2 A_2^{\alpha_2})(N - S) - \delta S. \tag{4.2}$$

In the Vidale–Wolfe model, each competitor's advertising is used in the attempt to attract market sales S, which are then divided between the two competitors according to the brand-strength parameters γ_1, γ_2. The market sales level changes dynamically according to equation (4.2). The maximum sales level is N, and the difference between the maximum and the current sales level is approachable through advertising. In addition to the buildup

65

in sales through advertising, there is also a decay at the rate of δ times the current level of sales. The parameters h_1, h_2 are the unit contributions of competitors 1 and 2, respectively, and r is the common discount rate.

We assume, as before, that the competitors are unable to cooperate in their advertising efforts. We wish, therefore, to pursue Nash equilibrium solutions. Both open-loop and closed-loop solutions are examined.

Open-Loop Solution

The Hamiltonians for the problem in equations (4.1)–(4.2) are

$$H_1 = h_1 \frac{\gamma_1}{\gamma_1 + \gamma_2} S - A_1 - k_1[(\beta_1 A_1^{\alpha_1} + \beta_2 A_2^{\alpha_2})(N - S) - \delta S]$$

$$H_2 = h_2 \frac{\gamma_1}{\gamma_1 + \gamma_2} S - A_2 - k_2[(\beta_1 A_1^{\alpha_1} + \beta_2 A_2^{\alpha_2})(N - S) - \delta S]. \quad (4.3)$$

The costate variables are subject to the dynamic constraints

$$\dot{k}_1 = rk_1 - \frac{\partial H_1}{\partial S} = (r + \delta + \beta_1 A_1^{\alpha_1} + \beta_2 A_2^{\alpha_2})k_1 - h_1 \frac{\gamma_1}{\gamma_1 + \gamma_2}$$

$$\dot{k}_2 = rk_2 - \frac{\partial H_2}{\partial S} = (r + \delta + \beta_1 A_1^{\alpha_1} + \beta_2 A_2^{\alpha_2})k_2 - h_2 \frac{\gamma_2}{\gamma_1 + \gamma_2}. \quad (4.4)$$

Setting $\partial H_1/\partial A_1 = 0$ and $\partial H_2/\partial A_2 = 0$ yields the following relationships that must hold in the solution:

$$k_1 = \frac{A_1^{1-\alpha_1}}{\alpha_1 \beta_1 (N - S)}$$

$$k_2 = \frac{A_2^{1-\alpha_2}}{\alpha_2 \beta_2 (N - S)}. \quad (4.5)$$

We can examine advertising in steady-state conditions by setting $\dot{S} = \dot{k}_1 = \dot{k}_2 = 0$. (This is equivalent to having $\dot{S} = \dot{A}_1 = \dot{A}_2 = 0$.) Setting $\dot{S} = 0$ yields

$$S = \frac{N(\beta_1 A_1^{\alpha_1} + \beta_2 A_2^{\alpha_2})}{\delta + \beta_1 A_1^{\alpha_1} + \beta_2 A_2^{\alpha_2}} \quad (4.6)$$

from which

$$N - S = \frac{\delta N}{\delta + \beta_1 A_1^{\alpha_1} + \beta_2 A_2^{\alpha_2}}. \quad (4.7)$$

Setting $\dot{k}_1 = 0$ yields

$$k_1 = \frac{h_1\gamma_1}{(\gamma_1 + \gamma_2)(r + \delta + \beta_1 A_1^{\alpha_1} + \beta_2 A_2^{\alpha_1})}. \tag{4.8}$$

Also, we have from equations (4.5) and (4.7) that

$$k_1 = \frac{A_1^{1-\alpha_1}(\delta + \beta_1 A_1^{\alpha_1} + \beta_2 A_2^{\alpha_2})}{\alpha_1\beta_1\delta N}. \tag{4.9}$$

Combining equations (4.8) and (4.9) implies the following advertising relationship:

$$A_1^{1-\alpha_1} = \frac{h_1\gamma_1\alpha_1\beta_1\delta N}{(\gamma_1 + \gamma_2)(r + \delta + \beta_1 A_1^{\alpha_1} + \beta_2 A_2^{\alpha_2})(\delta + \beta_1 A_1^{\alpha_1} + \beta_2 A_2^{\alpha_2})}. \tag{4.10}$$

Similarly, setting $\dot{k}_2 = 0$ yields the following relationship for A_2:

$$A_2^{1-\alpha_2} = \frac{h_2\gamma_2\alpha_2\beta_2\delta N}{(\gamma_1 + \gamma_2)(r + \delta + \beta_1 A_1^{\alpha_1} + \beta_2 A_2^{\alpha_2})(\delta + \beta_1 A_1^{\alpha_1} + \beta_2 A_2^{\alpha_2})}. \tag{4.11}$$

Dividing equation (4.10) by equation (4.11) produces the following relationship involving competitive advertising in steady state:

$$\frac{A_1^{1-\alpha_1}}{A_2^{1-\alpha_2}} = \frac{h_1\gamma_1\alpha_1\beta_1}{h_2\gamma_2\alpha_2\beta_2}. \tag{4.12}$$

If we have equal elasticity values $\alpha_1 = \alpha_2 = \alpha$, we have the following result for relative advertising in steady state:

$$\frac{A_1}{A_2} = \left(\frac{h_1\gamma_1\beta_1}{h_2\gamma_2\beta_2}\right)^{1/(1-\alpha)}. \tag{4.13}$$

That is, in steady state, relative advertising of the two competitors depends directly on the relative values of key parameters: unit contribution (h_1/h_2), brand strength (γ_1/γ_2), and advertising effectiveness (β_1/β_2). Finally, it should be noted that, in this Vidale–Wolfe formulation, relative sales of the two competitors is simply γ_1/γ_2, at any point in time, steady state or otherwise.

Closed-Loop Solution

We wish also to examine closed-loop solutions for the Vidale–Wolfe duopoly, i.e., advertising strategies $A_1(S)$, $A_2(S)$ that are functions of the level of sales. To find closed-loop solutions, consider the Hamiltonians (4.3) and value functions $V_1(S)$, $V_2(S)$ such that

$$V_1'(S) = k_1$$
$$V_2'(S) = k_2. \tag{4.14}$$

Maximizing the Hamiltonians with respect to advertising yields the following relationships:

$$V_1'(S) = \frac{A_1^{1-\alpha_1}(S)}{\alpha_1\beta_1(N - S)}$$

$$V_2'(S) = \frac{A_2^{1-\alpha_2}(S)}{\alpha_2\beta_2(N - S)} \tag{4.15}$$

from which

$$V_1(S) = \int^S \frac{A_1^{1-\alpha_1}(s)}{\alpha_1\beta_1(N - s)} ds$$

$$V_2(S) = \int^S \frac{A_2^{1-\alpha_2}(s)}{\alpha_2\beta_2(N - s)} ds \tag{4.16}$$

and we have the following Hamilton–Jacobi equations, expressed in terms of A_1, A_2, and S:

$$h_1 \frac{\gamma_1}{\gamma_1 + \gamma_2} S - A_1 + \frac{A_1^{1-\alpha_1}}{\alpha_1\beta_1(N - S)}[(\beta_1 A_1^{\alpha_1} + \beta_2 A_2^{\alpha_2})(N - S) - \delta S]$$

$$= r \int^S \frac{A_1^{1-\alpha_1}(s)}{\alpha_1\beta_1(N - S)} ds + c_1$$

$$h_2 \frac{\gamma_2}{\gamma_1 + \gamma_2} S - A_2 + \frac{A_1^{1-\alpha_2}}{\alpha_2\beta_2(N - S)}[(\beta_1 A_1^{\alpha_1} + \beta_2 A_2^{\alpha_2})(N - S) - \delta S]$$

$$= r \int^S \frac{A_2^{1-\alpha_2}(s)}{\alpha_2\beta_2(N - S)} ds + c_2 \tag{4.17}$$

for arbitrary constants c_1, c_2. Equations (4.17) are differentiable in S, and lead to the following system of differential equations in standard form (the derivation is shown in appendix 4.1):

$$A_1' = B^{-1}\left(\frac{1 - \alpha_2}{A_2}\dot{S}C - \frac{\alpha_2\beta_2}{A_2^{1-\alpha_2}}(N - S)D\right)$$

$$A_2' = B^{-1}\left(\frac{1 - \alpha_1}{A_1}\dot{S}D - \frac{\alpha_1\beta_1}{A_1^{1-\alpha_1}}(N - S)C\right) \tag{4.18}$$

where $\dot{S}$ is as in equation (4.2) and

$$B = \frac{1 - \alpha_1}{A_1}\frac{1 - \alpha_2}{A_2}\dot{S}^2 - \frac{\alpha_1\beta_1}{A_1^{1-\alpha_1}}\frac{\alpha_2\beta_2}{A_2^{1-\alpha_2}}(N - S)^2$$

$$C = r + \delta\frac{N}{N - S} - \frac{h_1\gamma_1\alpha_1\beta_1(N - S)}{(\gamma_1 + \gamma_2)A_1^{1-\alpha_1}}$$

$$D = r + \delta\frac{N}{N - S} - \frac{h_2\gamma_2\alpha_2\beta_2(N - S)}{(\gamma_1 + \gamma_2)A_2^{1-\alpha_2}}. \tag{4.19}$$

Assume that the discount rate $r = 0$. With this assumption, we have the following system of equations:

$$h_1\frac{\gamma_1}{\gamma_1 + \gamma_2}S - A_1 + \frac{A_1^{1-\alpha_1}}{\alpha_1\beta_1(N - S)}\dot{S} = c_1$$

$$h_2\frac{\gamma_2}{\gamma_1 + \gamma_2}S - A_2 + \frac{A_2^{1-\alpha_2}}{\alpha_2\beta_2(N - S)}\dot{S} = c_2. \tag{4.20}$$

To focus on steady-state relationships involving competitive advertising, note that equations (4.20) become, when $\dot{S} = 0$,

$$h_1\frac{\gamma_1}{\gamma_1 + \gamma_2}S - A_1 = c_1$$

$$h_2\frac{\gamma_2}{\gamma_1 + \gamma_2}S - A_2 = c_2 \tag{4.21}$$

and that

$$A_1 = h_1\frac{\gamma_1}{\gamma_1 + \gamma_2}S - c_1$$

$$A_2 = h_2\frac{\gamma_2}{\gamma_1 + \gamma_2}S - c_2. \tag{4.22}$$

Define

$$AR = \frac{A_1}{A_2} = \frac{h_1[\gamma_1/(\gamma_1 + \gamma_2)]S - c_1}{h_2[\gamma_2/(\gamma_1 + \gamma_2)]S - c_2}. \tag{4.23}$$

We wish to study how AR responds to changes in the parameters of the problem, and to compare the response patterns to those for open-loop solutions. Since the steady-state advertising ratio AR depends on the level of S, in general, we need to examine how S in steady state responds to changes in the prameters.

For equation (4.2), $\dot{S} = 0$ implies

$$
\begin{aligned}
S &= \frac{N(\beta_1 A_1^{\alpha_1} + \beta_2 A_2^{\alpha_2})}{\delta + \beta_1 A_1^{\alpha_1} + \beta_2 A_2^{\alpha_2}} \\
&= \frac{N\langle\beta_1\{h_1[\gamma_1/(\gamma_1 + \gamma_2)]S - c_1\}^{\alpha_1} + \beta_2\{h_2[\gamma_2/(\gamma_1 + \gamma_2)]S - c_2\}^{\alpha_2}\rangle}{\delta + \beta_1\{h_1[\gamma_1/(\gamma_1 + \gamma_2)]S - c_1\}^{\alpha_1} + \beta_2\{h_2[\gamma_2/(\gamma_1 + \gamma_2)]S - c_2\}^{\alpha_2}}
\end{aligned}
$$

(4.24)

which defines S implicitly in terms of the various parameters. Taking partial derivates leads to the following relationships:

$$
\frac{\partial S}{\partial N} = G^{-1}\left[\beta_1\left(h_1\frac{\gamma_1}{\gamma_1 + \gamma_2}S - c_1\right)^{\alpha_1} + \beta_2\left(h_2\frac{\gamma_2}{\gamma_1 + \gamma_2}S - c_2\right)^{\alpha_2}\right]
$$

$$
\cdot\left[\delta + \beta_1\left(h_1\frac{\gamma_1}{\gamma_1 + \gamma_2}S - c_1\right)^{\alpha_1} + \beta_2\left(h_2\frac{\gamma_2}{\gamma_1 + \gamma_2}S - c_2\right)^{\alpha_2}\right]
$$

$$
\frac{\partial S}{\partial \delta} = -G^{-1}N\left[\beta_1\left(h_1\frac{\gamma_1}{\gamma_1 + \gamma_2}S - c_1\right)^{\alpha_1} + \beta_2\left(h_2\frac{\gamma_2}{\gamma_1 + \gamma_2}S - c_2\right)^{\alpha_2}\right]
$$

$$
\frac{\partial S}{\partial \alpha_1} = G^{-1}N\delta\beta_1\left(h_1\frac{\gamma_1}{\gamma_1 + \gamma_2}S - c_1\right)^{\alpha_1}\ln\left(h_1\frac{\gamma_1}{\gamma_1 + \gamma_2}S - c_1\right)
$$

$$
\frac{\partial S}{\partial \alpha_2} = G^{-1}N\delta\beta_2\left(h_2\frac{\gamma_2}{\gamma_1 + \gamma_2}S - c_2\right)^{\alpha_2}\ln\left(h_2\frac{\gamma_2}{\gamma_1 + \gamma_2}S - c_2\right)
$$

$$
\frac{\partial S}{\partial \beta_1} = G^{-1}N\delta\left(h_1\frac{\gamma_1}{\gamma_1 + \gamma_2}S - c_1\right)^{\alpha_1}
$$

$$
\frac{\partial S}{\partial \beta_2} = G^{-1}N\delta\left(h_2\frac{\gamma_2}{\gamma_1 + \gamma_2}S - c_2\right)^{\alpha_2}
$$

$$
\frac{\partial S}{\partial \gamma_1} = G^{-1}NS\delta\frac{\gamma_2}{(\gamma_1 + \gamma_2)^2}
$$

$$
\cdot\left[h_1\alpha_1\beta_1\left(h_1\frac{\gamma_1}{\gamma_1 + \gamma_2}S - c_1\right)^{\alpha_1-1} - h_2\alpha_2\beta_2\left(h_2\frac{\gamma_2}{\gamma_1 + \gamma_2}S - c_2\right)^{\alpha_2-1}\right]
$$

$$\frac{\partial S}{\partial \gamma_2} = -G^{-1}NS\delta \frac{\gamma_1}{(\gamma_1 + \gamma_2)^2}$$

$$\cdot \left[h_1 a_1 \beta_1 \left(h_1 \frac{\gamma_1}{\gamma_1 + \gamma_2} S - c_1 \right)^{a_1-1} - h_2 a_2 \beta_2 \left(h_2 \frac{\gamma_2}{\gamma_1 + \gamma_2} S - c_2 \right)^{a_2-1} \right]$$

$$\frac{\partial S}{\partial h_1} = G^{-1}NS\delta a_1 \beta_1 \frac{\gamma_1}{\gamma_1 + \gamma_2} \left(h_1 \frac{\gamma_1}{\gamma_1 + \gamma_2} S - c_1 \right)^{a_1-1}$$

$$\frac{\partial S}{\partial h_2} = G^{-1}NS\delta a_2 \beta_2 \frac{\gamma_2}{\gamma_1 + \gamma_2} \left(h_2 \frac{\gamma_2}{\gamma_1 + \gamma_2} S - c_2 \right)^{a_2-1} \tag{4.25}$$

where

$$G = \delta^2 + \left[\beta_1 \left(h_1 \frac{\gamma_1}{\gamma_1 + \gamma_2} S - c_1 \right)^{a_1} + \beta_2 \left(h_2 \frac{\gamma_2}{\gamma_1 + \gamma_2} S - c_2 \right)^{a_2} \right]^2$$

$$+ \delta\beta_1 \left(h_1 \frac{\gamma_1}{\gamma_1 + \gamma_2} S - c_1 \right)^{a_1-1} \left[2\left(h_1 \frac{\gamma_1}{\gamma_1 + \gamma_2} S - c_1 \right) - \frac{Nh_1 a_1 \gamma_1}{\gamma_1 + \gamma_2} \right]$$

$$+ \delta\beta_2 \left(h_2 \frac{\gamma_2}{\gamma_1 + \gamma_2} S - c_2 \right)^{a_2-1} \left[2\left(h_2 \frac{\gamma_2}{\gamma_1 + \gamma_2} S - c_2 \right) - \frac{Nh_2 a_2 \gamma_2}{\gamma_1 + \gamma_2} \right].$$

The sign that G takes on depends on the value of S. While the sign of G is unclear over much of S, G is certainly positive if the following holds:

$$S > \max \left(\frac{Na_1}{2} + \frac{c_1(\gamma_1 + \gamma_2)}{h_1 \gamma_1}, \frac{Na_2}{2} + \frac{c_2(\gamma_1 + \gamma_2)}{h_2 \gamma_2} \right). \tag{4.26}$$

When G is positive, and assuming advertising for each competitor is strictly positive at steady state, we have the following proposition regarding the responsiveness to steady-state sales to the parameters:

Proposition 4.1. Assume that $G > 0$, steady-state $A_1 = h_1(\gamma_1/[\gamma_1 + \gamma_2]) \cdot S - c_1 > 0$, and steady-state $A_2 = h_2(\gamma_2/[\gamma_1 + \gamma_2])S - c_2 > 0$. Then the following hold, for S in steady state:

1. $\partial S/\partial N \geq 0$
2. $\partial S/\partial \delta \leq 0$
3. $\partial S/\partial a_1 \geq 0$ if, in addition, $S \geq (c_1 + 1)(\gamma_1 + \gamma_2)/h_1 \gamma_1$
4. $\partial S/\partial a_2 \geq 0$ if, in addition, $S \geq (c_2 + 1)(\gamma_1 + \gamma_2)/h_2 \gamma_2$
5. $\partial S/\partial \beta_1 \geq 0$
6. $\partial S/\partial \beta_2 \geq 0$
7. $\partial S/\partial h_1 \geq 0$

8. $\partial S/\partial h_2 \geq 0$
9. $\gamma_1(\partial S/\partial \gamma_1) = -\gamma_2(\partial S/\partial \gamma_2)$.

Proof. The proof follows directly from the assumptions and the relationships in (4.25).

Proposition 4.1 indicates that, for certain (large) values of S, at least, the steady-state sales level increases with increases in the potential sales level N, elasticities α_1, α_2, advertising effectiveness parameters β_1, β_2, and unit margins h_1, h_2. Also, steady-state S responds negatively to an increase in δ, the decay parameter. Finally, steady-state sales may respond either positively or negatively to a change in the brand-strength parameter γ_1, but the response is of the opposite sign of that for a change in the brand-strength parameter for competitor 2, γ_2. It is interesting in particular that an increase in the brand strength of one of the brands may lead to either an increase or a decrease in total market sales.

Now let us examine how the parameters affect the steady-state advertising ratio AR. From equation (4.23), we have that

$$\partial AR/\partial S = \frac{c_1 h_2 \gamma_2 - c_2 h_1 \gamma_1}{(\gamma_1 + \gamma_2)\{h_2[\gamma_2/(\gamma_1 + \gamma_2)]S - c_2\}^2}$$

$$\geq 0 \text{ if and only if } \frac{c_1}{h_1 \gamma_1} \geq \frac{c_2}{h_2 \gamma_2} \qquad (4.27)$$

assuming that steady-state advertising for competitor 2, $A_2 = h_2(\gamma_2/[\gamma_1 + \gamma_2])S - c_2$, is strictly positive. Using the relationship in equation (4.27) as well as the results in proposition 4.1, we have the following proposition relating the steady-state advertising ratio to changes in the parameters:

Proposition 4.2. Assume G, from relationships (4.25), > 0, steady-state $A_1 > 0$, and steady-state $A_2 > 0$. Then we have the following:

1. If $\partial AR/\partial S \geq 0$, $\partial AR/\partial N \geq 0$
2. If $\partial AR/\partial S \geq 0$, $\partial AR/\partial \delta \leq 0$
3. If $\partial AR/\partial S \geq 0$, and $S \geq (c_1 + 1)(\gamma_1 + \gamma_2)/h_1 \gamma_1$, $\partial AR/\partial \alpha_1 \geq 0$
4. If $\partial AR/\partial S \geq 0$, and $S \geq (c_2 + 1)(\gamma_1 + \gamma_2)/h_2 \gamma_2$, $\partial AR/\partial \alpha_2 \geq 0$
5. If $\partial AR/\partial S \geq 0$, $\partial AR/\partial \beta_1 \geq 0$
6. If $\partial AR/\partial S \leq 0$, $\partial AR/\partial \beta_2 \leq 0$ (although if $\partial AR/\partial S \geq 0$, $\partial AR/\partial \beta_2 \geq 0$)
7. If $\partial AR/\partial S \geq 0$, $\partial AR/\partial h_1 \geq 0$
8. If $\partial AR/\partial S \leq 0$, $\partial AR/\partial h_2 \leq 0$

9. If $\partial AR/\partial S \geqslant 0$, and $\partial S/\partial \gamma_1 \geqslant 0$, $\partial AR/\partial \gamma_1 \geqslant 0$
10. If $\partial AR/\partial S \geqslant 0$, and $\partial S/\partial \gamma_1 \geqslant 0$, $\partial AR/\partial \gamma_2 \leqslant 0$.

Proof. See appendix 4.2.

The results in proposition 4.2 can be compared to those for open-loop solutions. Recall relationship (4.13), which shows that for open-loop solutions, assuming $\alpha_1 = \alpha_2$, the ratio of steady-state advertising levels (competitor 1's advertising divided by competitor 2's) is related positively to h_1, γ_1, and β_1, and is related negatively to h_2, γ_2, and β_2. Results 5 through 10 of proposition 4.2 indicate that there are conditions under which the closed-loop steady-state advertising ratio responds in a similar fashion as the open-loop ratio. Of course, proposition 4.2 also shows, in results 1 through 4, that the closed-loop ratio is also responsive to parameters of the problem that do not enter into the open-loop ratio. Although there are some similarities in the way advertising ratios may respond, there are also differences between closed-loop and open-loop solutions in terms of steady-state advertising ratios. The primary reason for the differences is that closed-loop solutions depend functionally on the sales sate variable, and are subject to the responsiveness of steady-state sales to parameters.

Example

A specific example can be instructive for observing dynamic patterns of both closed-loop and open-loop solutions. For the example, assume the following set of parameter values:

$$r = 0$$
$$N = 1$$
$$\delta = .1$$
$$\alpha_1 = \alpha_2 = .5$$
$$\beta_1 = \beta_2 = .5$$
$$h_1 = h_2 = 1$$
$$\gamma_1 = \gamma_2 = \gamma \text{ (an arbitrary positive value)}$$
$$c_1 = c_2 = c \text{ (which will vary).} \quad (4.28)$$

With this set of parameter values, closed-loop advertising for the two competitors must satisfy

$$A_1 - \frac{2}{5}\frac{S}{1-S}\sqrt{A_2} + 2\sqrt{A_1 A_2} = c - \frac{S}{2}$$

$$A_2 - \frac{2}{5}\frac{S}{1-S}\sqrt{A_2} + 2\sqrt{A_1 A_2} = c - \frac{S}{2}. \tag{4.29}$$

Solutions for which $A_1 = A_2 = A$ can satisfy equations (4.29). A systematic search failed to find any solutions to equations (4.29) for which $A_1 \neq A_2$. This should not be a surprise, given the structure of the model and the symmetry in the parameters. As a consequence, the following acts as a solution:

$$A\ (= A_1 = A_2) = \left(\frac{2S/5(1-S) + \sqrt{4S^2/25(1-S)^2 - 6S + 12c}}{6}\right)^2. \tag{4.30}$$

The solution (4.30) is mapped in figure 4.1 for six values of c: $c = 0, .1,$ .2 in figure 4.1a, and $c = .3, .4, .5$ in figure 4.1b. All six curves show decline for small values of S and an increase for large values of S, approaching infinity as S approaches 1. Beyond this, however, there are distinct differences between the solutions shown in figure 4.1a and those in figure 4.1b. For each of $c = 0, .1, .2$, there is a portion of the curve (that portion shown lying on the abcissa) that is undefined; for a middling portion of each curve, there are no real values of A that satisfy equation (4.30). The curve for each of $c = .3, .4, .5$, on the other hand, is well defined for all values of $S \in [0, 1]$. However, it is also the case that these solutions have no steady-state values of S in the range $[0, 1]$, while those for $c = 0, .1, .2$ have two each. (See appendix 4.3 for details.) We concentrate, therefore, on closed-loop solutions for small values of c.

The dynamics of closed-loop sales and advertising, for a starting value for sales of $S = 0$, are shown in figure 4.2. Sales and advertising are determined numerically, period by period, by applying equation (4.30) for advertising and

$$\Delta S = \frac{\sqrt{A_1} + \sqrt{A_2}}{2}(1 - S) - \frac{S}{10} = \sqrt{A}(1 - S) - \frac{S}{10} \tag{4.31}$$

for the change in sales. Two values of c are shown. (For $c = 0$, sales and advertising stay at zero, a steady state.) For each of the solutions, advertising (equal for each competitor) declines toward a small, but nonzero, steady-state level, while the level of sales rises smoothly toward a steady-state value, which is approximately .201 for $c = .1$ and .410 for $c = .2$.

Not shown are the dynamics of sales and advertising for sales starting at

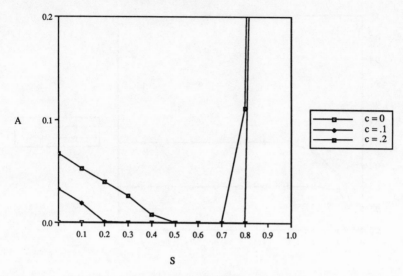

Figure 4.1a.   Closed-loop Equilibrium Advertising Strategies.

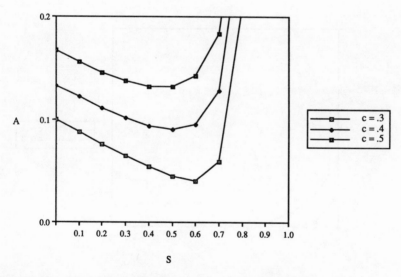

Figure 4.1b.   Closed-Loop Equilibrium Advertising Strategies.

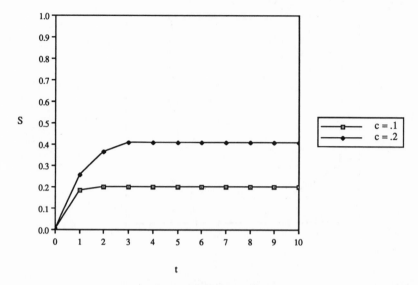

Figure 4.2a.   Closed-Loop Equilibrium Sales Paths.

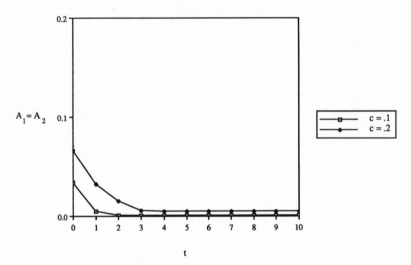

Figure 4.2b.   Closed-Loop Equilibrium Advertising Paths.

a relatively large level. For each $c = 0, .1, .2$, there is a second steady-state level of sales (approximately .868 for $c = 0$, .851 for $c = .1$, and .821 for $c = .2$). Numerical analysis shows that the larger steady-state level in each case can be achieved only by starting at that point. Starting at a slightly smaller value leads sales and advertising downward toward the indeterminate zone indicated in figure 4.1a. Starting at a slightly larger value than the steady-state sales level leads to ever larger values of advertising and sales; as S approaches 1, advertising approaches infinity. *If sales are at a relatively high level, there is an inherent lack of stability that is not resolved, unless the situation is already at steady state.* Although this may not be very appealing in theory, it may explain certain actual situations in which the competitors appear to become involved in an escalating advertising war.

For comparison, the open-loop solution is shown in figure 4.3. (See appendix 4.4 for the details involved in finding the solution.) For S starting at zero, sales climb toward a steady-state value of approximately .6305. (Numerical analysis shows that S tends toward the same steady-state value whatever the starting point.) Also, advertising, equal for the two competitors in this example, declines monotonically toward a steady-state value of approximately .0291.

Caution is needed in drawing conclusions from the numerical study of a single example. However, some interesting patterns develop from the example studied in the present chapter. The pattern of increasing sales and decreasing advertising across time is common to both open-loop and closed-loop solutions, as long as the closed-loop soluton has a small value of the constant c and if S starts at a low level. Indeed, a closed-loop solution can be found that closely resembles the open-loop solution. Figure 4.4 shows the closed-loop solution for $c = .2862$, and S starting at zero. While there are some differences in the approach to steady state, sales and advertising are almost identical once steady state is reached. Steady-state profits are essentially equal for this closed-loop solution and the open-loop solution. Closed-loop solutions can be found that have higher profits in steady state, but only in a narrow range of the parameter c. The largest value of c for which a steady state is possible is, to four decimal places, .2955; this is also the largest steady-state profit each competitor can obtain. This profit level is only about 3.3% larger than that for the open-loop solution.

Comparison of Closed-Loop and Open-Loop Solutions

The example indicates that there may be dynamic similarities between open-loop and closed-loop solutions for the Vidale–Wolfe model. For

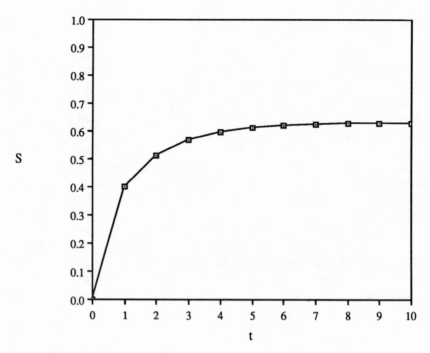

Figure 4.3a. Open-Loop Equilibrium Sales Path.

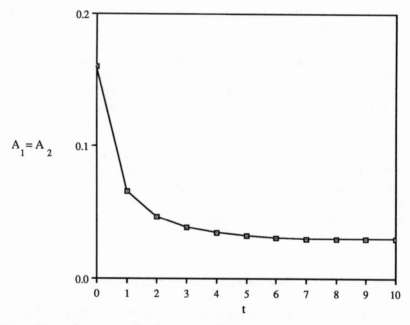

Figure 4.3b. Open-Loop Equilibrium Advertising Path.

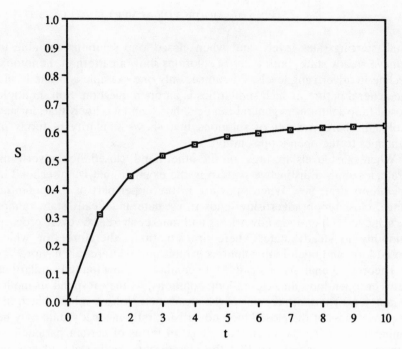

Figure 4.4a.   Closed-Loop Equilibrium Sales Path, $c = .2862$.

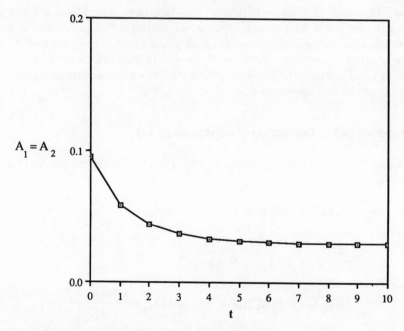

Figure 4.4b.   Closed-Loop Equilibrium Advertising Path, $c = .2862$.

small starting sales levels, and when closed-loop solutions are able to achieve steady state, both types of solutions show a pattern of monotonic decline in advertising levels. Of course, only one example is offered, and the general nature of such similarities is an open question. Still, multiple closed-loop solutions in general can be defined, and it is likely that, for any problem, there is a set of solutions that shows similarity in terms of dynamics to the open-loop solution.

When sales levels are high, on the other hand, closed-loop advertising strategies show a distinctive pattern in the example that is not echoed in open-loop strategies. When sales are in the upper part of the potential range, closed-loop advertising tends to escalate and steady state cannot be achieved. Open-loop advertising and market share, however, proceed smoothly to steady state. There are situations, therefore, for which closed-loop and open-loop solutions exhibit quite different behavior.

Theoretical analysis of steady-state conditions show limited similarities between open-loop and closed-loop solutions, as they respond to model parameters. There are regions of the steady-state sales level for which the responsiveness of the closed-loop advertising ratio in steady state may be similar to that for the open-loop ratio, in terms of certain parameters. However, it is also shown that the closed-loop steady-state advertising ratio depends on the parameters N and δ, while the open-loop ratio does not. The basic difference between open-loop and closed-loop solutions, that in the latter advertising depends on the level of sales while in the former advertising depends on time alone, dictates the differences that appear. For closed-loop solutions, if the steady-state sales level is dependent upon a particular parameter, then, therefore, so are the advertising levels of the two competitors.

Appendix 4.1. Derivation of equations (4.18)

Define B, C, D as in equations (4.19). Differentiating equations (4.17) produces

$$\frac{1 - \alpha_1}{A_1}[(\beta_1 A_1^{\alpha_1} + \beta_2 A_2^{\alpha_2})(N - S) - \delta S]A_1' + \frac{\alpha_2 \beta_2 (N - S)}{A_2^{1-\alpha_2}}A_2'$$

$$= r + \delta \frac{N}{N - S} - \frac{h_1 \gamma_1 \alpha_1 \beta_1 (N - S)}{(\gamma_1 + \gamma_2)A_1^{1-\alpha_1}}$$

$$\frac{1 - \alpha_2}{A_2}[(\beta_1 A_1^{\alpha_1} + \beta_2 A_2^{\alpha_2})(N - S) - \delta S]A_2' + \frac{\alpha_1 \beta_1 (N - S)}{A_1^{1-\alpha_1}}A_1'$$

$$= r + \delta\frac{N}{N - S} - \frac{h_2\gamma_2\alpha_2\beta_2(N - S)}{(\gamma_1 + \gamma_2)A_2^{1-\alpha_2}} \tag{A4.1}$$

or

$$\frac{1 - \alpha_1}{A_1}\dot{S}A_1' + \frac{\alpha_2\beta_2(N - S)}{A_2^{1-\alpha_2}}A_2' = C$$

$$\frac{1 - \alpha_2}{A_2}\dot{S}A_2' + \frac{\alpha_1\beta_1(N - S)}{A_1^{1-\alpha_1}}A_1' = D. \tag{A4.2}$$

In matrix form,

$$\begin{bmatrix} \dfrac{1 - \alpha_1}{A_1}\dot{S} & \dfrac{\alpha_2\beta_2(N - S)}{A_2^{1-\alpha_2}} \\[3mm] \dfrac{\alpha_1\beta_1(N - S)}{A_1^{1-\alpha_1}} & \dfrac{1 - \alpha_2}{A_2}\dot{S} \end{bmatrix}\begin{bmatrix} A_1' \\[2mm] A_2' \end{bmatrix} = \begin{bmatrix} C \\[2mm] D \end{bmatrix} \tag{A4.3}$$

so that

$$\begin{bmatrix} A_1' \\[2mm] A_2' \end{bmatrix} = \left(\frac{1 - \alpha_1}{A_1}\frac{1 - \alpha_2}{A_2}\dot{S}^2 - \frac{\alpha_1\beta_1}{A_1^{1-\alpha_1}}\frac{\alpha_2\beta_2}{A_2^{1-\alpha_2}}(N - S)^2\right)^{-1}$$

$$\cdot\begin{bmatrix} \dfrac{1 - \alpha_2}{A_2}\dot{S} & \dfrac{-\alpha_2\beta_2(N - S)}{A_2^{1-\alpha_2}} \\[3mm] \dfrac{-\alpha_1\beta_1(N - S)}{A_1^{1-\alpha_1}} & \dfrac{1 - \alpha_1}{A_1}\dot{S} \end{bmatrix}\begin{bmatrix} C \\[2mm] D \end{bmatrix}$$

$$= B^{-1}\begin{bmatrix} \dfrac{1 - \alpha_2}{A_2}\dot{S} & \dfrac{-\alpha_2\beta_2(N - S)}{A_2^{1-\alpha_2}} \\[3mm] \dfrac{-\alpha_1\beta_1(N - S)}{A_1^{1-\alpha_1}} & \dfrac{1 - \alpha_1}{A_1}\dot{S} \end{bmatrix}\begin{bmatrix} C \\[2mm] D \end{bmatrix}. \tag{A4.4}$$

Appendix 4.2. Proof of proposition 4.2

Assume $G > 0$, $h_1[\gamma_1/(\gamma_1 + \gamma_2)]S - c_1 > 0$, and $h_2[\gamma_2/(\gamma_1 + \gamma_2)]S - c_2 > 0$. Results 1 through 6 in proposition 4.2 follow directly from proposition 4.1 and the fact that $\partial AR/\partial x = (\partial AR/\partial S)(\partial S/\partial x)$ for $x = n, \delta, \alpha_1, \alpha_2, \beta_1, \beta_1$. For result 7, note that

$$\frac{\partial AR}{\partial h_1} = \frac{(\gamma_1/[\gamma_1 + \gamma_2])S}{h_2[\gamma_2/(\gamma_1 + \gamma_2)]S - c_2} + \frac{\partial AR}{\partial S}\frac{\partial S}{\partial h_1}$$

$$\geq 0 \text{ if } \frac{\partial AR}{\partial S} \geq 0. \tag{A4.5}$$

For result 8,

$$\frac{\partial AR}{\partial h_2} = \frac{-[\gamma_2/(\gamma_1 + \gamma_2)]\{h_1[\gamma_1/(\gamma_1 + \gamma_2)]S - c_1\}S}{\{h_2[\gamma_2/(\gamma_1 + \gamma_2)]S - c_2\}^2} + \frac{\partial AR}{\partial S}\frac{\partial S}{\partial h_2}$$

$$\leq 0 \text{ if } \frac{\partial AR}{\partial S} \leq 0. \tag{A4.6}$$

For result 9, we calculate that

$$\frac{\partial AR}{\partial \gamma_1} = \frac{\begin{aligned}&[h_1\gamma_2/(\gamma_1 + \gamma_2)^2]\{h_2[\gamma_2/(\gamma_1 + \gamma_2)]S - c_2\}S\\&+ [h_2\gamma_2/(\gamma_1 + \gamma_2)^2]\{h_1[\gamma_1/(\gamma_1 + \gamma_2)]S - c_1\}S\\&+ [(c_1h_2\gamma_2 - c_2h_1\gamma_1)/(\gamma_1 + \gamma_2)](\partial S/\partial \gamma_1)\end{aligned}}{\{h_2[\gamma_2/(\gamma_1 + \gamma_2)]S - c_2\}^2}$$

$$= \frac{\begin{aligned}&[h_1\gamma_2/(\gamma_1 + \gamma_2)^2]\{h_2[\gamma_2/(\gamma_1 + \gamma_2)]S - c_2\}S\\&+ [h_2\gamma_2/(\gamma_1 + \gamma_2)^2]\{h_1[\gamma_1/(\gamma_1 + \gamma_2)]S - c_1\}S\end{aligned}}{\{h_2[\gamma_2/(\gamma_1 + \gamma_2)]S - c_2\}^2} + \frac{\partial AR}{\partial S}\frac{\partial S}{\partial \gamma_1}$$

$$\geq 0 \text{ if } \frac{\partial AR}{\partial S} \geq 0 \text{ and } \frac{\partial S}{\partial \gamma_1} \geq 0. \tag{A4.7}$$

Finally, for result 10,

$$\frac{\partial AR}{\partial \gamma_2} = -\frac{\begin{aligned}&[h_1\gamma_1/(\gamma_1 + \gamma_2)^2]\{h_2[\gamma_2/(\gamma_1 + \gamma_2)]S - c_2\}S\\&+ [h_2\gamma_1/(\gamma_1 + \gamma_2)^2]\{h_1[\gamma_1/(\gamma_1 + \gamma_2)]S - c_1]S\end{aligned}}{\{h_2[\gamma_2/(\gamma_1 + \gamma_2)]S - c_2\}^2} + \frac{\partial AR}{\partial S}\frac{\partial S}{\partial \gamma_2}$$

$$= -\frac{\begin{aligned}&[h_1\gamma_1/(\gamma_1 + \gamma_2)^2]\{h_2[\gamma_2/(\gamma_1 + \gamma_2)]S - c_2\}S\\&+ [h_2\gamma_1/(\gamma_1 + \gamma_2)^2]\{h_1[\gamma_1/(\gamma_1 + \gamma_2)]S - c_1\}S\end{aligned}}{\{h_2[\gamma_2/(\gamma_1 + \gamma_2)]S - c_2\}^2} - \frac{\gamma_1}{\gamma_2}\frac{\partial AR}{\partial S}\frac{\partial S}{\partial \gamma_1}$$

$$\leq 0 \text{ if } \frac{\partial AR}{\partial S} \geq 0 \text{ and } \frac{\partial S}{\partial \gamma_1} \geq 0. \tag{A4.8}$$

Appendix 4.3.   Steady-state sales levels for the example

With the parameter levels chosen for the example, the steady-state sales level can be derived from the following condition:

$$S = \frac{\sqrt{S/2} - c}{1/10 + \sqrt{S/2} - c,} \tag{A4.9}$$

which implies the following cubic relationship

$$f(S) = S^3 - 2(1.01 + c)S^2 + (1 + 4c)S - 2c = 0. \tag{A4.10}$$

For each value of $c = 0, .1, .2, .3, .4, .5$, a search for roots of the cubic in (A4.10) provides the following (rounded) values:

c	$f^{-1}(0)$
0	0, .868, 1.152
.1	.201, 851, 1.168
.2	.41, .821, 1.19
.3	1.22
.4	1.263
.5	1.328

Only $c = 0, .1, .2$ show roots in the range $[0, 1]$ for S, and there are exactly two such roots for each of those c. Inserting each such root in equation (A4.9) confirms that it indeed satisfies the condition for steady state.

Appendix 4.4.   Open-loop solution for the example

The Hamiltonians for the open-loop solution are

$$H_1 = \frac{h_1 S}{2} - A_1 + k_1 \dot{S}$$

$$H_2 = \frac{h_2 S}{2} - A_2 + k_2 \dot{S} \tag{A4.11}$$

where

$$\dot{S} = \frac{(\sqrt{A_1} + \sqrt{A_2})(1 - S)}{2} - \frac{S}{10} \tag{A4.12}$$

and

$$\dot{k}_1 = \frac{(1/5 + \sqrt{A_1} + \sqrt{A_2})k_1 - 1}{2}$$

$$\dot{k}_2 = \frac{(1/5 + \sqrt{A_1} + \sqrt{A_2})k_2 - 1}{2}. \qquad (A4.13)$$

Maximizing the Hamiltonians requires

$$A_1 = \left(\frac{k_1[1 - S]}{4}\right)^2$$

$$\qquad (A4.14)$$

$$A_2 = \left(\frac{k_2[1 - S]}{4}\right)^2.$$

At steady state, we have from equations (4.10) and (4.11) that

$$\sqrt{A_1} = \sqrt{A_2} = \frac{1}{80}\left(\frac{1}{10} + \frac{\sqrt{A_1}}{2} + \frac{\sqrt{A_2}}{2}\right)^{-2} \qquad (A4.15)$$

so that

$$\sqrt{A_1} = \frac{1}{80}\left(\frac{1}{10} + \sqrt{A_1}\right)^{-2}. \qquad (A4.16)$$

Algebraic manipulation of equation (A4.16) leads to the following relationship:

$$80A_1^{3/2} + 16A_1 + \frac{4}{5}A_1^{1/2} - 1 = 0. \qquad (A4.17)$$

There is exactly one real root for $A_1^{1/2}$ in equation (A4.17), $A_1^{1/2} \simeq .1706$. This leads to

$$k_1 = k_2 \simeq 1.847. \qquad (A4.18)$$

The open-loop solution is derived through the following algorithm:

1. Set the initial value $S(0)$. Also, set terminal values $k_1(T)$, $k_2(T)$ from equation (A4.18).
2. Choose beginning values $A_1(t)$, $A_2(t)$ for $t = 1, 2, \ldots, T$.
3. For $t = 1, 2, \ldots, T$, determine $S(t)$ through forward integration, using equation (A4.12).
4. For $t = T - 1, T - 2, \ldots 0$, determine $k_1(t)$, $k_2(t)$ through backward integration, using equations (A4.13).

5. For $t = 1, 2, \ldots, T$, determine $A_1(t)$, $A_2(t)$ through equations (A4.14). If, for each $t = 1, 2, \ldots, T$, $A_1(t)$ and $A_2(t)$ are sufficiently close to the corresponding values for the previous iteration, stop. Otherwise, return to step 3.

5 ANALYSIS OF A DIFFUSION DUOPOLY

The final model we analyze is the diffusion (with repeat) formulation. With this model, we assume, again, that the two competitors in the duopoly wish to maximize discounted profits over an infinite horizon:

$$\max_{A_1} \int^{\infty} e^{-rt}\left(h_1 \frac{\gamma_1}{\gamma_1 + \gamma_2} S - A_1\right) dt$$

$$\max_{A_1} \int_0^{\infty} e^{-rt}\left(h_2 \frac{\gamma_2}{\gamma_1 + \gamma_2} S - A_2\right) dt \qquad (5.1)$$

The dynamic constraint on sales in the diffusion model is

$$\dot{S} = (\beta_1 A_1^{\alpha_1} + \beta_2 A_2^{\alpha_2} + \varepsilon S)(N - S) - \delta S. \qquad (5.2)$$

The model is similar to the Vidale–Wolfe structure analyzed in chapter 4, with the exception of the word-of-mouth parameter ε. As before, r is the discount rate, h_1, h_2 are the unit contributions of the two competitors, γ_1, γ_2 are brand-strength parameters, α_1, α_2 are advertising elasticities, β_1, β_2 are advertising-effectiveness parameters, δ is a decay factor, and N is the maximum market size.

Open-Loop Solution

An open-loop solution to the diffusion model (5.1)–(5.2) is obtained by maximizing the Hamiltonians

$$H_1 = h_1 \frac{\gamma_1}{\gamma_1 + \gamma_2} S - A_1 - k_1([\beta_1 A_1^{\alpha_1} + \beta_2 A_2^{\alpha_2} + \varepsilon S][N - S] - \delta S)$$

$$H_2 = h_2 \frac{\gamma_2}{\gamma_1 + \gamma_2} S - A_2 - k_2([\beta_1 A_1^{\alpha_1} + \beta_2 A_2^{\alpha_2} + \varepsilon S][N - S] - \delta S).$$

$$(5.3)$$

The costate variables vary across time according to

$$\dot{k}_1 = rk_1 - \frac{\partial H_1}{\partial S} = (r + \delta + \varepsilon[2S - N] + \beta_1 A_1^{\alpha_1} + \beta_2 A_2^{\alpha_2})k_1 - h_1 \frac{\gamma_1}{\gamma_1 + \gamma_2}$$

$$\dot{k}_2 = rk_2 - \frac{\partial H_2}{\partial S} = (r + \delta + \varepsilon[2S - N] + \beta_1 A_1^{\alpha_1} + \beta_2 A_2^{\alpha_2})k_2 - h_2 \frac{\gamma_2}{\gamma_1 + \gamma_2}.$$

$$(5.4)$$

Setting $\partial H_1/\partial A_1 = 0$ and $\partial H_2/\partial A_2 = 0$ yields

$$k_1 = \frac{A_1^{1-\alpha_1}}{\alpha_1 \beta_1 (N - S)}$$

$$k_2 = \frac{A_2^{1-\alpha_2}}{\alpha_2 \beta_2 (N - S)}.$$

$$(5.5)$$

In steady state, $\dot{k}_1 = \dot{k}_2 = 0$, and therefore

$$k_1 = \frac{A_1^{1-\alpha_1}}{\alpha_1 \beta_1 (N - S)} = \frac{h_1 \gamma_1}{(\gamma_1 + \gamma_2)[r + \delta + \varepsilon(2S - N) + \beta_1 A_1^{\alpha_1} + \beta_2 A_2^{\alpha_2}]}$$

$$k_2 = \frac{A_2^{1-\alpha_2}}{\alpha_2 \beta_2 (N - S)} = \frac{h_2 \gamma_2}{(\gamma_1 + \gamma_2)[r + \delta + \varepsilon(2S - N) + \beta_1 A_1^{\alpha_1} + \beta_2 A_2^{\alpha_2}]}$$

$$(5.6)$$

for S in steady state. From equations (5.6),

$$\frac{A_1^{1-\alpha_1}}{A_2^{1-\alpha_2}} = \frac{\alpha_1 \beta_1 h_1 \gamma_1}{\alpha_2 \beta_2 h_2 \gamma_2}.$$

$$(5.7)$$

If we have $\alpha_1 = \alpha_2 = \alpha$, then the ratio of advertising levels of the two competitors in steady state is

$$\frac{A_1}{A_2} = \left(\frac{\beta_1 h_1 \gamma_1}{\beta_2 h_2 \gamma_2}\right)^{1/(1-\alpha)}, \tag{5.8}$$

which is the same result as that for the Vidale–Wolfe model. This is due to the similarity between the two models. Only the word-of-mouth parameter ε separates the two models (4.2) and (5.2), and nothing is added to the diffusion model from the Vidale–Wolfe model that varies for the two competitors. For both models, the steady-state open-loop advertising ratio is a function of relative advertising effectiveness (β_1/β_2), relative unit contribution (h_1/h_2), and relative brand strength (γ_1/γ_2).

Closed-Loop Solution

To find closed-loop solutions to the diffusion model, we identify value functions through the substitutions

$$V_1'(S) = k_1$$
$$V_2'(S) = k_2 \tag{5.9}$$

in the Hamiltonians H_1, H_2 in equations (5.3). Setting $\partial H_1/\partial A_1$ and $\partial H_2/\partial A_2$ to zero yields

$$V_1'(S) = \frac{A_1^{1-\alpha_1}}{\alpha_1\beta_1(N-S)}$$

$$V_2'(S) = \frac{A_2^{1-\alpha_2}}{\alpha_2\beta_2(N-S)} \tag{5.10}$$

and

$$V_1(S) = \int^S \frac{A_1^{1-\alpha_1}(s)}{\alpha_1\beta_1(N-s)}\,ds$$

$$V_2(S) = \int^S \frac{A_2^{1-\alpha_2}(s)}{\alpha_2\beta_2(N-s)}\,ds. \tag{5.11}$$

Solutions to the following equations provide closed-loop advertising strategies, in terms of the sales level S:

$$h_1\frac{\gamma_1}{\gamma_1+\gamma_2}S - A_1 + \frac{A_1^{1-\alpha_1}}{\alpha_1\beta_1(N-S)}[(\beta_1 A_1^{\alpha_1} + \beta_2 A_2^{\alpha_2} + \varepsilon S)(N-S) - \delta S]$$

$$= r\int^S \frac{A_1^{1-\alpha_1}(s)}{\alpha_1\beta_1(N-s)}\,ds + c_1$$

$$h_2 \frac{\gamma_2}{\gamma_1 + \gamma_2} S - A_2 + \frac{A_2^{1-\alpha_2}}{\alpha_2 \beta_2 (N - S)} [(\beta_1 A_1^{\alpha_1} + \beta_2 A_2^{\alpha_2} + \varepsilon S)(N - S) - \delta S]$$

$$= r \int^S \frac{A_2^{1-\alpha_2}(s)}{\alpha_2 \beta_2 (N - S)} ds + c_2. \tag{5.12}$$

Differentiation produces the following system of differential equations expressed in standard form:

$$A_1' = B^{-1} \left(\frac{1 - \alpha_2}{A_2} \dot{S} C - \frac{\alpha_2 \beta_2}{A_2^{1-\alpha_2}} (N - S) D \right)$$

$$A_2' = B^{-1} \left(\frac{1 - \alpha_1}{A_1} \dot{S} D - \frac{\alpha_1 \beta_1}{A_1^{1-\alpha_1}} (N - S) C \right) \tag{5.13}$$

where $\dot{S}$ is defined in equation (5.2) and

$$B = \frac{1 - \alpha_1}{A_1} \frac{1 - \alpha_2}{A_2} \dot{S}^2 - \frac{\alpha_1 \beta_1}{A_1^{1-\alpha_1}} \frac{\alpha_2 \beta_2}{A_2^{1-\alpha_2}} (N - S)^2$$

$$C = r + \delta \frac{N}{N - S} - \varepsilon(N - S) - h_1 \frac{\gamma_1}{\gamma_1 + \gamma_2} \frac{\alpha_1 \beta_1}{A_1^{1-\alpha_1}} (N - S)$$

$$D = r + \delta \frac{N}{N - S} - \varepsilon(N - S) - h_2 \frac{\gamma_1}{\gamma_1 + \gamma_2} \frac{\alpha_2 \beta_2}{A_2^{1-\alpha_2}} (N - S). \tag{5.14}$$

Details of the derivation of equations (5.14) are in appendix 5.1.
   If $r = 0$, the system (5.12) becomes

$$h_1 \frac{\gamma_1}{\gamma_1 + \gamma_2} S - A_1 + \frac{A_1^{1-\alpha_1}}{\alpha_1 \beta_1 (N - S)} [(\beta_1 A_1^{\alpha_1} + \beta_2 A_2^{\alpha_2} + \varepsilon S)(N - S) - \delta S] = c_1$$

$$h_2 \frac{\gamma_2}{\gamma_1 + \gamma_2} S - A_2 + \frac{A_2^{1-\alpha_2}}{\alpha_2 \beta_2 (N - S)} [(\beta_1 A_1^{\alpha_1} + \beta_2 A_2^{\alpha_2} + \varepsilon S)(N - S) - \delta S] = c_2.$$

$$\tag{5.15}$$

At steady state, $\dot{S} = 0$, we have the following relationships for the two competitors' advertising:

$$A_1 = h_1 \frac{\gamma_1}{\gamma_1 + \gamma_2} S - c_1$$

$$A_2 = h_2 \frac{\gamma_2}{\gamma_1 + \gamma_2} S - c_2 \tag{5.16}$$

and

$$AR = \frac{A_1}{A_2} = \frac{h_1[\gamma_1/(\gamma_1 + \gamma_2)]S - c_1}{h_2[\gamma_2/(\gamma_1 + \gamma_2)]S - c_2}. \tag{5.17}$$

Also, setting $\dot{S} = 0$ in equation (5.2) yields the following relationship for steady-state sales:

$$S = \frac{1}{2\varepsilon}[-\beta_1 A_1^{\alpha_1} - \beta_2 A_2^{\alpha_2} - \delta + \varepsilon N$$
$$+ \sqrt{(\beta_1 A_1^{\alpha_1} + \beta_2 A_2^{\alpha_2})^2 + (\delta - \varepsilon N)^2 + 2(\delta + \varepsilon N)(\beta_1 A_1^{\alpha_1} + \beta_2 A_2^{\alpha_2})}] \tag{5.18}$$

where the (steady-state) levels of A_1 and A_2 are determined by equations (5.16).

Comparative static analysis of sales and the advertising ratio in steady state offers modest insights. We do have that

$$\frac{\partial S}{\partial N} = G^{-1}\left(1 + \frac{\beta_1 A_1^{\alpha_1} + \beta_2 A_2^{\alpha_2} + \varepsilon N - \delta}{K}\right)$$

$$\frac{\partial S}{\partial \varepsilon} = G^{-1}\frac{1}{\varepsilon}\left[N + (\beta_1 A_1^{\alpha_1} + \beta_2 A_2^{\alpha_2})\left(\frac{N}{K} + \frac{1}{\varepsilon}\right) + (\varepsilon N - \delta)\left(\frac{N}{K} - \frac{1}{\varepsilon}\right) - \frac{K}{\varepsilon}\right]$$

$$\frac{\partial S}{\partial \delta} = G^{-1}\frac{1}{\varepsilon}\left(\frac{\beta_1 A_1^{\alpha_1} + \beta_2 A_2^{\alpha_2} - \varepsilon N + \delta}{K} - 1\right)$$

$$\frac{\partial S}{\partial \alpha_1} = G^{-1}\frac{1}{\varepsilon}\left(\frac{\beta_1 A_1^{\alpha_1} + \beta_2 A_2^{\alpha_2} + \varepsilon N + \delta}{K} - 1\right)\beta_1 A_1^{\alpha_1}\ln A_1$$

$$\frac{\partial S}{\partial \alpha_2} = G^{-1}\frac{1}{\varepsilon}\left(\frac{\beta_1 A_1^{\alpha_1} + \beta_2 A_2^{\alpha_2} + \varepsilon N + \delta}{K} - 1\right)\beta_2 A_2^{\alpha_2}\ln A_2$$

$$\frac{\partial S}{\partial \beta_1} = G^{-1}\frac{1}{\varepsilon}\left(\frac{\beta_1 A_1^{\alpha_1} + \beta_2 A_2^{\alpha_2} + \varepsilon N + \delta}{K} - 1\right)A_1^{\alpha_1}$$

$$\frac{\partial S}{\partial \beta_2} = G^{-1}\frac{1}{\varepsilon}\left(\frac{\beta_1 A_1^{\alpha_1} + \beta_2 A_2^{\alpha_2} + \varepsilon N + \delta}{K} - 1\right)A_1^{\alpha_2}$$

$$\frac{\partial S}{\partial \gamma_1} = G^{-1}\frac{1}{\varepsilon}\left(\frac{\beta_1 A_1^{\alpha_1} + \beta_2 A_2^{\alpha_2} + \varepsilon N + \delta}{K} - 1\right)\left(\frac{h_1\alpha_1\beta_1}{A_1^{1-\alpha_1}} - \frac{h_2\alpha_2\beta_2}{A_2^{1-\alpha_2}}\right)\frac{\gamma_2}{(\gamma_1 + \gamma_2)^2}S$$

$$\frac{\partial S}{\partial \gamma_2} = G^{-1}\frac{1}{\varepsilon}\left(\frac{\beta_1 A_1^{\alpha_1} + \beta_2 A_2^{\alpha_2} + \varepsilon N + \delta}{K} - 1\right)\left(\frac{h_2\alpha_2\beta_2}{A_2^{1-\alpha_2}} - \frac{h_1\alpha_1\beta_1}{A_1^{1-\alpha_1}}\right)\frac{\gamma_1}{(\gamma_1 + \gamma_2)^2}S$$

$$\frac{\partial S}{\partial h_1} = G^{-1} \frac{1}{\varepsilon} \left(\frac{\beta_1 A_1^{\alpha_1} + \beta_2 A_2^{\alpha_2} + \varepsilon N + \delta}{K} - 1 \right) \frac{\alpha_1 \beta_1}{A_1^{1-\alpha_1}} \frac{\gamma_1}{\gamma_1 + \gamma_2} S$$

$$\frac{\partial S}{\partial h_2} = G^{-1} \frac{1}{\varepsilon} \left(\frac{\beta_1 A_1^{\alpha_1} + \beta_2 A_2^{\alpha_2} + \varepsilon N + \delta}{K} - 1 \right) \frac{\alpha_2 \beta_2}{A_2^{1-\alpha_2}} \frac{\gamma_2}{\gamma_1 + \gamma_2} S \qquad (5.19)$$

where

$$K = \sqrt{(\beta_1 A_1^{\alpha_1} + \beta_2 A_2^{\alpha_2})^2 + (\delta - \varepsilon N)^2 + 2(\delta + \varepsilon N)(\beta_1 A_1^{\alpha_1} + \beta_2 A_2^{\alpha_2})}$$

and

$$G = 2 - \frac{1}{\varepsilon} \left(\frac{\beta_1 A_1^{\alpha_1} + \beta_2 A_2^{\alpha_2} + \varepsilon N + \delta}{K} - 1 \right) \frac{(h_1 \gamma_1 \alpha_1 \beta_1 / A_1^{1-\alpha_1} + h_2 \gamma_2 \alpha_2 \beta_2 / A_2^{1-\alpha_2})}{\gamma_1 + \gamma_2}.$$

We also have that

$$\frac{\partial AR}{\partial S} = \frac{c_1 h_2 \gamma_2 - c_2 h_1 \gamma_1}{(\gamma_1 + \gamma_2) A_2^2} \qquad (5.20)$$

and that

$$\frac{\partial AR}{\partial N} = \frac{\partial AR}{\partial S} \frac{\partial S}{\partial N}$$

$$\frac{\partial AR}{\partial \varepsilon} = \frac{\partial AR}{\partial S} \frac{\partial S}{\partial \varepsilon}$$

$$\frac{\partial AR}{\partial \delta} = \frac{\partial AR}{\partial S} \frac{\partial S}{\partial \delta}$$

$$\frac{\partial AR}{\partial \alpha_1} = \frac{\partial AR}{\partial S} \frac{\partial S}{\partial \alpha_1}$$

$$\frac{\partial AR}{\partial \alpha_2} = \frac{\partial AR}{\partial S} \frac{\partial S}{\partial \alpha_2}$$

$$\frac{\partial AR}{\partial \beta_1} = \frac{\partial AR}{\partial S} \frac{\partial S}{\partial \beta_1}$$

$$\frac{\partial AR}{\partial \beta_2} = \frac{\partial AR}{\partial S} \frac{\partial S}{\partial \beta_2}$$

$$\frac{\partial AR}{\partial \gamma_1} = \frac{\gamma_2 S(h_1 A_2 + h_2 A_1)}{(\gamma_1 + \gamma_2)^2 A_2^2} + \frac{\partial AR}{\partial S} \frac{\partial S}{\partial \gamma_1}$$

$$\frac{\partial AR}{\partial \gamma_2} = \frac{-\gamma_1 S(h_1 A_2 + h_2 A_1)}{(\gamma_1 + \gamma_2)^2 A_2^2} + \frac{\partial AR}{\partial S} \frac{\partial S}{\partial \gamma_2}$$

$$\frac{\partial AR}{\partial h_1} = \frac{\gamma_1 S}{(\gamma_1 + \gamma_2)A_2} + \frac{\partial AR}{\partial S}\frac{\partial S}{\partial h_1}.$$

$$\frac{\partial AR}{\partial h_2} = \frac{-\gamma_2 S A_1}{(\gamma_1 + \gamma_2)A_2^2} + \frac{\partial AR}{\partial S}\frac{\partial S}{\partial h_2}. \tag{5.21}$$

Unfortunately, G in equations (5.19) is of equivocal sign, and general conclusions cannot be drawn regarding the direction of the response of sales and the advertising ratio to changes in the parameters. It is clear from equations (5.19)–(5.21), however, that, in general, the closed-loop steady-state advertising ratio is different in nature from the open-loop ratio in that the closed-loop ratio is responsive to all the parameters, not just to h_1, h_2, γ_1, γ_2, β_1, and β_2.

Example

Numerical analysis of a specific example will be used to indicate how the word-of-mouth parameter ε affects advertising strategies, and to compare open-loop and closed-loop solutions in this regard. Recall that the diffusion model is similar to the Vidale–Wolfe formulation studied in chapter 4; the models differ only in the word-of-mouth effect that is added to the diffusion model. The specific parameter values assumed for the example are

$$r = 0$$
$$N = 1$$
$$\delta = .1$$
$$\alpha_1 = \alpha_2 = .5$$
$$\beta_1 = \beta_2 = .5$$
$$\gamma_1 = \gamma_2 = \gamma \text{ (an arbitrary value)}$$
$$h_1 = h_2 = 1. \tag{5.22}$$

Closed-loop equilibria patterns for varying values of $c = c_1 = c_2$ are very similar to those for the Vidale–Wolfe example in chapter 4. Nothing is gained, therefore, from such an examination in the present chapter. The distinguishing feature of the diffusion model is the word-of-mouth parameter ε, and it is interesting to note the variation in the dynamic behavior of both the open-loop and closed-loop solutions as that parameter is varied. In what follows, for each value of ε examined, the

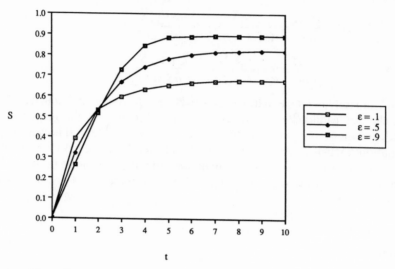

Figure 5.1a.   Open-Loop- Equilibrium Sales Paths.

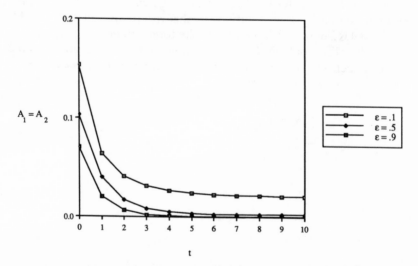

Figure 5.1b.   Open-Loop Equilibrium Advertising Paths.

closed-loop solution shown is the one that most closely resembles the open-loop equilibrium.

Open-loop solutions for three values of ε are shown in figure 5.1. (Details on derivation of the solutions are in appendix 5.2) The starting sales level is zero in each case. It is evident that the competitors feel less need to advertise with an increasing word-of-mouth effect. In each case, advertising levels for both competitors decline monotonically over time, but advertising is consistently at lower levels for higher values of the ε parameter. This is reflected in the sales pattern, which shows slower initial growth for higher values of ε. As steady state is approached, however, sales are higher with larger word-of-mouth effects, even though advertising levels are relatively low. The larger steady-state sales levels, and the smaller steady-state advertising levels, are due purely to the greater ability to attract current noncustomers through word of mouth.

For each value of ε, a closed-loop solution is derived that attains the same steady-state sales level as the open-loop solution. (Details of derivation of the closed-loop solutions are in appendix 5.3.) This required differing values of c for the closed-loop solutions, $c \simeq .3189, .4082,$ and $.4453$ for $\varepsilon = .1, .5, .9$, respectively. The dynamics of the closed-loop solutions, for sales starting at the zero level, are shown in figure 5.2. There are similarities with open-loop solutions, in that advertising levels tend to decline across time, and are lower in the approach to steady state with increasing values of the word-of-mouth parameter ε. The difference is in the initial period levels for advertising. As ε increases, closed-loop advertising in the initial period becomes larger, rather than smaller as for open-loop equilibria. For closed-loop equilibria, the sales level both grows faster in the early periods and approaches a larger steady-state level when the word-of-mouth effect becomes larger.

Comparison of Closed-Loop and Open-Loop Solutions

For any particular problem, there are a number of closed-loop solutions that can be defined. The example indicates that it may be possible to find a closed-loop solution that closely resembles the open-loop solution, at least in terms of steady-state levels of sales and advertising. Further, although sales and advertising in the transition to steady state differ in terms of precise levels, both the open-loop and the chosen closed-loop solutions exhibit monotonically growing sales and declining advertising, although only when initial sales are low. When the initial sales level is higher than the open-loop steady-state level, all similarities between open-loop and

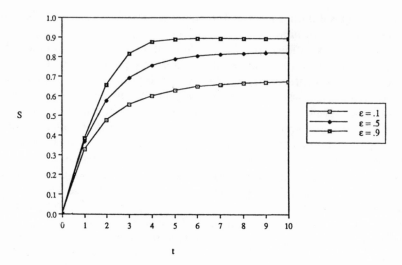

Figure 5.2a.   Closed-Loop Equilibrium Sales Paths.

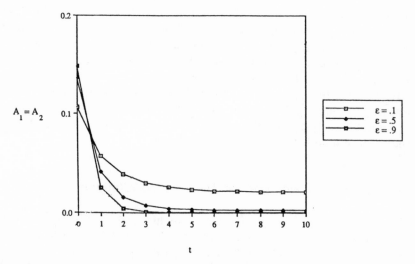

Figure 5.2b.   Closed-Loop Equilibrium Advertising Paths.

closed-loop solutions disappear. Numerical analyses (not shown) show a consistent pattern for open-loop solutions—declining sales and increasing advertising in the approach to steady state. For closed-loop solutions, however, one of three patterns can occur: 1) if the initial sales level is in a limited region above the steady-state level, both sales and advertising show decline toward steady state; 2) the sales level begins in or enters a region for which closed-loop solutions are not defined; 3) advertising levels for the two competitors grow toward infinity. The last situation occurs for initial sales levels in the upper part of the $[0, N]$ range. This pattern also occurs for the Vidale–Wolfe model. It would appear that for both the Vidale–Wolfe model and the more general diffusion model, there is a high possibility of unstable or undefinable advertising levels for the two competitors, if market sales are at a high level.

In addition, the theoretical analysis, although limited for the diffusion model, indicates differences in the way advertising in steady state depends on parameter levels. For open-loop solutions, the steady-state advertising ratio between the two competitors depends only on a limited number of parameters. Closed-loop steady-state advertising ratios, on the other hand, since they depend on the sales level, are subject in general to variation in any of the parameters.

Appendix 5.1. Derivation of equations (5.14)

Differentiating in equations (5.12) produces

$$
\frac{1 - \alpha_1}{A_1} \dot{S} A_1' + \frac{\alpha_2 \beta_2}{A_2^{1-\alpha_2}} (N - S) A_2'
$$

$$
= r + \delta \frac{N}{N - S} - \varepsilon(N - S) - h_1 \frac{\gamma_1}{\gamma_1 + \gamma_2} \frac{\alpha_1 \beta_1}{A_1^{1-\alpha_1}} (N - S)
$$

$$
= C
$$

$$
\frac{1 - \alpha_2}{A_2} \dot{S} A_2' + \frac{\alpha_1 \beta_1}{A_1^{1-\alpha_1}} (N - S) A_1'
$$

$$
= r + \delta \frac{N}{N - S} - \varepsilon(N - S) - h_2 \frac{\gamma_2}{\gamma_1 + \gamma_2} \frac{\alpha_2 \beta_2}{A_2^{1-\alpha_2}} (N - S)
$$

$$
= D. \tag{A5.1}
$$

Expressed in matrix form,

$$\begin{bmatrix} \dfrac{1-\gamma_1}{A_1}\dot{S} & \dfrac{\alpha_2\beta_2}{A_2^{1-\alpha_2}}(N-S) \\[2ex] \dfrac{\alpha_1\beta_1}{A_1^{1-\alpha_1}}(N-S) & \dfrac{1-\gamma_2}{A_2}\dot{S} \end{bmatrix}\begin{bmatrix} A_1' \\ A_2' \end{bmatrix} = \begin{bmatrix} C \\ D \end{bmatrix} \tag{A5.2}$$

and, therefore, that

$$\begin{bmatrix} A_1' \\ A_2' \end{bmatrix} = \left(\frac{1-\alpha_1}{A_1}\frac{1-\alpha_2}{A_2}\dot{S}^2 - \frac{\alpha_1\beta_1}{A_1^{1-\alpha_1}}\frac{\alpha_2\beta_2}{A_2^{1-\alpha_2}}(N-S)^2 \right)^{-1}$$

$$\cdot \begin{bmatrix} \dfrac{1-\gamma_2}{A_2}\dot{S} & -\dfrac{\alpha_2\beta_2}{A_2^{1-\alpha_2}}(N-S) \\[2ex] -\dfrac{\alpha_1\beta_1}{A_1^{1-\alpha_1}}(N-S) & \dfrac{1-\gamma_1}{A_1}\dot{S} \end{bmatrix}\begin{bmatrix} C \\ D \end{bmatrix}$$

$$= B^{-1}\begin{bmatrix} \dfrac{1-\gamma_2}{A_2}\dot{S} & -\dfrac{\alpha_2\beta_2}{A_2^{1-\alpha_2}}(N-S) \\[2ex] -\dfrac{\alpha_1\beta_1}{A_1^{1-\alpha_1}}(N-S) & \dfrac{1-\gamma_1}{A_1}\dot{S} \end{bmatrix}\begin{bmatrix} C \\ D \end{bmatrix}. \tag{A5.3}$$

Appendix 5.2.   Open-loop solutions for the example

The Hamiltonians for the open-loop solutions are

$$H_1 = \frac{S}{2} - A_1 + k_1\left[\left(\frac{\sqrt{A_1}}{2} + \frac{\sqrt{A_2}}{2} + \varepsilon S\right)(1-S) - \frac{S}{10}\right]$$

$$H_2 = \frac{S}{2} - A_2 + k_2\left[\left(\frac{\sqrt{A_1}}{2} + \frac{\sqrt{A_2}}{2} + \varepsilon S\right)(1-S) - \frac{S}{10}\right]. \tag{A5.4}$$

They dynamic constraints are

$$\dot{S} = \left(\frac{\sqrt{A_1}}{2} + \frac{\sqrt{A_2}}{2} + \varepsilon S\right)(1-S) - \frac{S}{10} \tag{A5.5}$$

and

$$\dot{k}_1 = \left(\frac{\sqrt{A_1}}{2} + \frac{\sqrt{A_2}}{2} + \varepsilon(2S-1) + \frac{1}{10}\right)k_1 - \frac{1}{2}$$

$$\dot{k}_2 = \left(\frac{\sqrt{A_1}}{2} + \frac{\sqrt{A_2}}{2} + \varepsilon(2S-1) + \frac{1}{10}\right)k_2 - \frac{1}{2}. \tag{A5.6}$$

Maximizing the Hamiltonians (A5.4) with respect to advertising requires

$$A_1 = \left(\frac{k_1(1 - S)}{4}\right)^2$$

$$A_2 = \left(\frac{k_2(1 - S)}{4}\right)^2. \tag{A5.7}$$

At steady state, $\dot{S} = \dot{k}_1 = \dot{k}_2 = 0$. This implies that

$$k_1 = k_2 = k = \frac{1}{2}\left(\frac{k(1 - S)}{4} + \varepsilon(2S - 1) + \frac{1}{10}\right) \tag{A5.8}$$

or that

$$k = \frac{1}{1 - S}\left[-2\left(\varepsilon(2S - 1) + \frac{1}{10}\right) + \sqrt{4\left(\varepsilon(2S - 1) + \frac{1}{10}\right)^2 + 2(1 - S)}\right]. \tag{A5.9}$$

(The positive root to the quadratic relationship created by equation (A5.8) is taken, and the negative root ignored, to ensure that the Hamiltonians are maximized, rather that minimized, at $\partial H/\partial A_1 = 0$ and $\partial H_2/\partial A_2 = 0$.) Also at steady state,

$$S = \frac{1}{2\varepsilon}\left[\frac{-k(1 - S)}{4} + \varepsilon - \frac{1}{10}\right.$$
$$\left. + \sqrt{\frac{k^2(1 - S)^2}{16} + \left(\frac{1}{10} - \varepsilon\right)^2 + \frac{(1/10 + \varepsilon)k(1 - S)}{2}}\right]. \tag{A5.10}$$

For each value of ε, a search is conducted to determine the (steady-state) value of k that satisfies the relationships in equations (A5.9) and (A5.10).

The open-loop solution is derived from the following algorithm:

1. Set the initial value $S(0)$. Also, set terminal values $k_1(T) = k_2(T)$ to satisfy equations (A5.9)–(A5.10).
2. Choose beginning values $A_1(t)$, $A_2(t)$ for $t = 1, 2, \ldots, T$.
3. For $t = 1, 2, \ldots, T$, determine $S(t)$ through forward integration, using equation (A5.5).
4. For $t = T - 1, T - 2, \ldots, 0$, determine $k_1(t)$, $k_2(t)$ through backward integration, using equations (A5.6).
5. For $t = 1, 2, \ldots, T$, determine $A_1(t)$, $A_2(t)$ through equations (A5.7). If, for each $t = 1, 2, \ldots, T$, $A_1(t)$ and $A_2(t)$ are sufficiently

close to the corresponding values for the previous iteration, stop. Otherwise, return to step 3.

Appendix 5.3.   Closed-loop solutions for the example

In the example, advertising levels, as functions of sales S, must satisfy the following system of equations:

$$A_1 + 4S\left(\varepsilon - \frac{1}{10(1 - S)}\right)\sqrt{A_1} + 2\sqrt{A_1 A_2} = c - \frac{S}{2}$$

$$A_2 + 4S\left(\varepsilon - \frac{1}{10(1 - S)}\right)\sqrt{A_2} + 2\sqrt{A_1 A_2} = c - \frac{S}{2}. \quad (A5.11)$$

Having $A_1 = A_2$ provides the following solution:

$$A_1 = A_2 = \left(\frac{-4S[\varepsilon - 1/10(1 - S)] + \sqrt{16S^2[\varepsilon - 1/10(1 - S)]^2 - 6S + 12c}}{6}\right)^2. \quad (A5.12)$$

The dynamics of the solution, for a particular starting sales level, are determined by applying equation (A5.12), updating S according to

$$\Delta S = \left(\frac{\sqrt{A_1}}{2} + \frac{\sqrt{A_2}}{2} + \varepsilon S\right)(1 - S) - \frac{S}{10} \quad (A5.13)$$

and repeating the sequence until ΔS is sufficiently small.

6 SUMMARY AND FINAL CONSIDERATIONS

In the last three chapters, we analyzed three different duopoly models of advertising competition. Before summarizing what has been learned in the analysis, there are two issues that need some discussion: 1) extension of the modeling to more than two competitors; and 2) empirical testing and validation of models.

Extension to more than two competitors

Complications are added when the number of competitors is greater than two, in particular if the number of state variables in the problem is increased. To illustrate, consider the triopoly version of the Lanchester model:

$$\max_{A_1} \int_0^\infty e^{-rt}(g_1 M_1 - A_1)dt$$

$$\max_{A_2} \int_0^\infty e^{-rt}(g_2 M_2 - A_2)dt$$

$$\max_{A_3} \int_0^\infty e^{-rt}[g_3(1 - M_1 - M_2) - A_3]dt \qquad (6.1)$$

where the two market-share state variables are subject to the following differential processes:

$$\dot{M}_1 = \beta_1 A_1^{\alpha_1}(1 - M_1) - (\beta_2 A_2^{\alpha_2} + \beta_3 A_3^{\alpha_3})M_1$$
$$\dot{M}_2 = \beta_2 A_2^{\alpha_2}(1 - M_2) - (\beta_1 A_1^{\alpha_1} + \beta_3 A_3^{\alpha_3})M_2. \qquad (6.2)$$

Without showing the details, we can derive the steady-state advertising levels of the three competitors:

$$A_1^{1-\alpha_1} = \frac{g_1\alpha_1\beta_1(\beta_2 A_2^{\alpha_2} + \beta_3 A_3^{\alpha_3})}{(\beta_1 A_1^{\alpha_1} + \beta_2 A_2^{\alpha_2} + \beta_3 A_3^{\alpha_3})(r + \beta_1 A_1^{\alpha_1} + \beta_2 A_2^{\alpha_2} + \beta_3 A_3^{\alpha_3})}$$

$$A_2^{1-\alpha_2} = \frac{g_2\alpha_2\beta_2(\beta_1 A_1^{\alpha_1} + \beta_3 A_3^{\alpha_3})}{(\beta_1 A_1^{\alpha_1} + \beta_2 A_2^{\alpha_2} + \beta_3 A_3^{\alpha_3})(r + \beta_1 A_1^{\alpha_1} + \beta_2 A_2^{\alpha_2} + \beta_3 A_3^{\alpha_3})}$$

$$A_3^{1-\alpha_3} = \frac{g_3\alpha_3\beta_3(\beta_1 A_1^{\alpha_1} + \beta_2 A_2^{\alpha_2})}{(\beta_1 A_1^{\alpha_1} + \beta_2 A_2^{\alpha_2} + \beta_3 A_3^{\alpha_3})(r + \beta_1 A_1^{\alpha_1} + \beta_2 A_2^{\alpha_2} + \beta_3 A_3^{\alpha_3})} \qquad (6.3)$$

Unfortunately, it does not appear that the relationships in equations (6.3) can be manipulated further to yield expressions for relative values of advertising that are defined explicitly in terms of problem parameters, as could be done in the duopoly case.

Nor are closed-loop results easy to derive. For one thing, the Hamilton–Jacobi equations cannot be expressed cleanly in terms of A_1, A_2, A_3, and M, to exclude value functions. In addition, the equations involve nonlinear partial differential equations. At steady state, advertising levels can be stated in terms of the market shares M_1, M_2:

$$A_1 = g_1 M_1 - c_1$$
$$A_2 = g_2 M_2 - c_2$$
$$A_3 = g_3(1 - M_1 - M_2) - c_3. \qquad (6.4)$$

However, the steady-state expressions that result for the market shares

$$M_1 = \frac{\beta_1(g_1 M_1 - c_1)^{\alpha_1}}{\beta_1(g_1 M_1 - c_1)^{\alpha_1} + \beta_2(g_2 M_2 - c_2)^{\alpha_2} + \beta_3[g_3(1 - M_1 - M_2) - c_3]^{\alpha_3}}$$

$$M_2 = \frac{\beta_2(g_2 M_2 - c_2)^{\alpha_1}}{\beta_1(g_1 M_1 - c_1)^{\alpha_1} + \beta_2(g_2 M_2 - c_2)^{\alpha_2} + \beta_3[g_3(1 - M_1 - M_2) - c_3]^{\alpha_3}}$$
$$(6.5)$$

are sufficiently complex to prevent straightforward conclusions regarding the effects of parameters on steady-state market shares and advertising levels.

The complications encountered in the triopoly version of the Lanchester model are due to having more than one state variable. Such problems are not experienced in m-player generalizations of the other two models studied, Vidale–Wolfe and diffusion, in that those models can maintain a single state variable. In the Vidale–Wolfe and diffusion models, as formulated, advertising by the various competitors does not determine market shares, but instead influences total industry sales. Consider an extension of the more general diffusion model to m competitors:

$$\max_{A_i} \int_0^\infty e^{-rt}\left[h_i\left(\gamma_i \bigg/ \sum_1^m \gamma_j\right)S - A_i\right]dt, \ i = 1, \ldots, m \qquad (6.6)$$

where

$$\dot{S} = \left(\sum_1^m \beta_j A_j^{\alpha_j} + \varepsilon S\right)(N - S) - \delta S. \qquad (6.7)$$

For open-loop strategies in steady state, it is easily shown that advertising levels bear the same relative relationships in the m-competitor model as that for a duopoly:

$$\frac{A_i^{1-\alpha_i}}{A_j^{1-\alpha_j}} = \frac{\alpha_i \beta_i h_i \gamma_i}{\alpha_j \beta_j h_j \gamma_j} \qquad (6.8)$$

and, if $\alpha_i = \alpha_j = \alpha$,

$$\frac{A_i}{A_j} = \left(\frac{\beta_i h_i \gamma_i}{\beta_j h_j \gamma_j}\right)^{1/(1-\alpha)}. \qquad (6.9)$$

Furthermore, closed-loop solutions are not difficult to identify. For a general, positive r, a system of ordinary differential equations in standard form can be obtained. If $r = 0$, solutions do not require evaluation of differential equations; a system of m equations in the m unknown functions of $S, A_1, \ldots, A_m$ results.

Empirical issues

Empirical validation of theoretical models of advertising competition is an important step in establishing the contribution of such models to the understanding of how advertising decisions are made in competitive markets. Empirical work to date on advertising competition, attempting to establish advertising effects on sales and market share as well as what may influence the advertising decisions of the competing firms, has tended not to be based on rigorous model development, certainly not in a differential game framework. The models advanced in the present monograph can be used as bases for empirical study. There are some econometric issues that need to be addressed for such work to be useful, however.

Proper estimation may involve a single equation, or it may involve a system of equations, depending on what we assume to be the basis for the competing firms' advertising decisions. If we believe that the competitors in a particular empirical application are adopting open-loop strategies, estimation need involve only a single equation, i.e., the appropriate dynamic market-share or sales model

$$\dot{M} = \beta_1 A_1^{\alpha_1}(1 - M) - \beta_2 A_2^{\alpha_2} M \qquad (3.3)$$

or

$$\dot{S} = (\beta_1 A_1^{\alpha_1} + \beta_2 A_2^{\alpha_2})(N - S) - \delta S \qquad (4.2)$$

or

$$\dot{S} = (\beta_1 A_1^{\alpha_1} + \beta_2 A_2^{\alpha_2} + \varepsilon S)(N - S) - \delta S \qquad (5.2)$$

(multiple equations would be needed if more than one state variable is modeled), to estimate the parameters driving the demand process in the market. Choosing the appropriate model—Lanchester (3.3), Vidale–Wolfe (4.2), or diffusion (5.2)—is best done by considering basic questions, perhaps aided by a preliminary look at the data. If the market is characterized by stable overall sales and a battle for market share, the Lanchester model is appropriate. If, on the other hand, total industry sales appear to be expanding through the advertising efforts of the competitors, then either the Vidale–Wolfe or the diffusion model would be better. As defined, the Vidale–Wolfe model is nested in the diffusion model, so a good approach would be to begin with the diffusion formulation, and test whether the Vidale–Wolfe model is more appropriate. The appropriate differential equation, (3.3), (4.2), or (5.2), would need to be discretized, and estimation would require nonlinear techniques.

If closed-loop strategies are used by the competitors, however, a *simultaneous system of equations* may need to be adopted. In a closed-loop situation, not only does market share or sales depend on advertising, but the competitors' advertising levels depend on market share/sales, as well. If the temporal interval in the data is fine enough, a *recursive* system may be adequate, in which advertising depends on lagged, but not current, levels of market share/sales, since actual reaction in terms of advertising spending is unlikely to occur instantaneously. However, certain situations need to assume simultaneous effects, e.g., if annual data are involved.

Whether a simultaneous or a recursive system is needed for closed-loop situations, estimating the advertising dependence on market share/sales can provide estimates of parameters that are often not known to the researcher, e.g., unit contributions, or indeed the constants c_1, c_2 in the Hamilton–Jacobi equations that define the closed-loop strategies. Consider a Lanchester duopoly. Under the constraints $r = 0$ and $\alpha_1 = \alpha_2 = .5$, i.e., changes in market share are proportional to the *square root* of advertising levels, we can express closed-loop advertising levels explicitly in terms of market share. If we define

$$G_1 = g_1 M - c_1$$
$$G_2 = g_2[1 - M] - c_2 \tag{6.10}$$

the following expressions result:

$$A_1 = \frac{2[M/(1-M)]^2(\beta_2/\beta_1)^2 G_2 - G_1 + 2\sqrt{G_1^2 - [M/(1-M)]^2(\beta_2/\beta_1)^2 G_1 G_2 + [M/(1-M)]^4(\beta_2/\beta_1)^4 G_2^2}}{3}$$

$$A_2 = \frac{2[(1-M)/M]^2(\beta_1/\beta_2)^2 G_1 - G_2 + 2\sqrt{G_2^2 - [(1-M)/M]^2(\beta_1/\beta_2)^2 G_1 G_2 + [(1-M)/M]^4(\beta_1/\beta_2)^4 G_1^2}}{3}$$

$$\tag{6.11}$$

For estimation, the equations in (6.11) would be combined in a (nonlinear) recursive or simultaneous system with a discrete version of equation (3.3), in which α_1 and α_2 are constrained to equal .5:

$$\Delta M = \beta_1 \sqrt{A_1}(1 - M) - \beta_2 \sqrt{A_2} M. \tag{6.12}$$

Significantly, empirical analysis can also help distinguish whether open-loop or closed-loop strategies are used by the competitors. If open-loop strategies are used, advertising varies across time, but as a function only of time itself. On the other hand, the perfect equilibrium concept of Case (1979) that is used to derive closed-loop strategies implies that advertising varies with market share, but is not otherwise dependent on time. An empirical test for open-loop versus closed-loop strategies is the following. For shorthand purposes, call the right-hand sides of the equations in (6.11) $f_1(M)$ and $f_2(M)$, respectively. The following equations could be estimated:

$$A_1 = w_{11} f_1(M) + w_{12} h_1(t)$$
$$A_2 = w_{21} f_2(M) + w_{22} h_2(t) \tag{6.13}$$

where $h_1(\cdot)$ and $h_2(\cdot)$ are some appropriate functions depicting the shape of the advertising trajectories through time (linear functions may suffice), $A_1 = A_1(t)$, $A_2 = A_2(t)$, and $M = M(t)$ if the advertising dependence on market share is simultaneous. If the market share–advertising relationship is recursive, we can have $M = M(t - 1)$ in equations (6.13). The w_{ij}, i, $j = 1, 2$, to be estimated, are weighting factors on closed-loop versus open-loop advertising strategies.

Estimation of the advertising relationships in equations (6.13), specifically the weights w_{ij}, can tell us the extent to which the competitors adopt closed-loop or open-loop strategies. For either competitor $i = 1, 2$, we have the following two scenarios of particular interest, which are stated as empirically testable propositions:

Proposition 6.1. Competitor i adopts a closed-loop advertising strategy. This is the case if $w_{i1} = 1$ and $w_{i2} = 0$.

Proposition 6.2. Competitor i adopts an open-loop advertising strategy. This is indicated by $w_{i1} = 0$. The open-loop parameter w_{i2} may $= 0$, which would indicate open-loop advertising that has achieved steady state.

Depending on the results of statistical hypothesis tests concerning the parameters w_{ij}, we can determine empirically whether a particular competitor uses an open-loop strategy, wherein advertising is not adjusted as market share varies, or a closed-loop strategy, which directly accounts for market share in updating advertising levels. It is also possible that a competitor may combine the two strategic approaches, to have a strategy that allows advertising to vary with *both* time and market share. This would indicate that a more general closed-loop strategy is involved:

Proposition 6.3. Competitor i adopts a general closed-loop strategy, in which advertising levels are a function of time as well as market share. This would be indicated if both w_{i1}, $w_{i2} \neq 0$.

We might expect that both competitors in a duopoly would use the same type of strategy, whether it be closed-loop or open-loop. This is a basic assumption that is made in deriving Nash equilibria for a differential game. However unlikely, it may be possible that the two adopt different strategies, one using a closed-loop strategy while the other adopts an open-loop one, perhaps due to differences in available information relating to market share. One firm may not be able to observe changing levels in market share due to a lack of reliable marketing research. In this case, we could have the following situation:

Proposition 6.4. One competitor, competitor i, adopts a closed-loop strategy, while the other, competitor j ($j \neq i$), adopts an open-loop strategy. This would be indicated by $w_{i1} \neq 0$ and $w_{j1} = 0$.

Finally, other competitive models could also be tested by adding appropriate variables to the right-hand sides of the relationships in (6.18). A possible leader–follower situation could be investigated, for example, by including lagged competitor advertising as an explanatory variable in the estimation.

Theoretical model development becomes useful when it can be established empirically that theoretical models are valid representations of actual competitive behavior. A strong argument can be made for competitors adjusting their advertising due to changing market conditions. However, it may also be the case that competitors are unable or unwilling to do so. As discussed in the review of empirical research in the opening chapter of the monograph, there currently is limited and mixed evidence regarding the dependence of advertising strategies on changing levels of sales or market shares. With the approach suggested in the present section, we have the ability to deal with this important issue on a more rigorous basis, to begin sorting out the extent to which competing advertisers use information on the current state of the market to modify their advertising strategies.

Summary and Future Directions

Theoretical analysis of the Lanchester, Vidale–Wolfe, and diffusion models show that open-loop and closed-loop solutions are quite different, at least in terms of steady-state conditions. Relative advertising levels of duopolistic competitors in steady state are influenced differently by model parameters under closed-loop versus open-loop strategies. The basis for the difference is that closed-loop strategies depend on a continuing basis upon current levels of market share or sales, while open-loop strategies do not.

A clear difference between the two types of strategy concepts is that there appear to be many more closed-loop solutions to a particular problem than there are open-loop solutions. The specific examples presented serve to indicate that it may often be possible to find a closed-loop strategy that closely resembles an open-loop strategy. Of course, it is also possible to find closed-loop strategies that look quite different from an open-loop solution to a particular problem. Furthermore, it appears from the examples that there are likely to be closed-loop strategies that return higher (steady-state) profits to the competitors than are available under an open-loop strategy, although the difference in profits may not be large, as is seen in the Vidale–Wolfe example.

We should, of course, be cautious about drawing general conclusions from specific examples. Nevertheless, there are certain patterns that emerge from the examples presented that are similar to those found in previous research. For instance, a market-share adjustment phenomenon, in which advertising is used to adjust a market share that is undesirably high or low, is found in the open-loop solution for the Lanchester example in chapter 3; this adjustment process is not always detected in closed-loop strategies for the example, however. For low initial sales levels in the Vidale–Wolfe and diffusion examples, both open-loop and closed-loop strategies show a pattern of declining advertising across time, a pattern frequently encountered in existing research. Note that this pattern is achieved herein without either a finite planning horizon or market satura-tion (where sales approach zero, as in the first-purchase-only diffusion models of Teng and Thompson (1983), Horsky and Mate (1988), and Dockner and Jørgensen (1990)). Further, the pattern of escalating adver-tising on the part of the competitors that develops when starting sales levels are high in the Vidale–Wolfe and diffusion examples may provide some support, and an alternative model, for the positive advertising inter-actions detected empirically by certain studies (Lambin 1970a; Grabowski and Mueller 1971; Metwally 1975). A final conclusion arising from the various examples studied is that, due to the abundance of closed-loop solutions available, strategies can be identified that indicate either positive or negative, or both (depending on the level of the share or sales state variable), effects of market share or sales on advertising levels. This provides a likely explanation for the lack of a consistently positive or negative effect in existing empirical studies.

Future research on competitive advertising models can proceed in two directions: analytical and empirical. Clearly, more could be learned about closed-loop solutions, in particular. However analytical extensions to in-clude more than one state variable, or to have closed-loop strategies vary with time as well as with state variables, requires analysis of partial dif-ferential equations, and a general theory for such an analysis has not been developed. For now, numerical methods may have to suffice.

Greater marginal benefit may come from empirical analysis, to gain a greater understanding of what competitive advertising strategies are being used in particular empirical applications. Potentially, a firm could adopt either an open-loop or a closed-loop strategy; if closed-loop, one of many possible could be chosen. It is not theoretically clear which strategy concept should be adopted, or how to choose among a large number of potential strategies. Ultimately, this is an empirical issue, and methods such as those discussed in the previous section can be useful in furthering our understanding of the competive use of dynamic advertising strategies.

The value of interpreting advertising competition in a differential game framework lies not only in its research implications. There are valuable managerial insights that can be obtained, as well, through a differential game interpretation. The explicit modeling of the dynamic nature of markets, and the implications for advertising not only at a single point in time but also as it changes with market share or sales and over time, allows a manager to plan for the future. Adopting a game theory approach encourages a manager to think in terms of a competitor's problem as well as his or her own. The Nash equilibria that derive from the differential game model can be viewed as potential, if not actual, outcomes that would develop if both the manager's firm and its competitor were attempting to maximize long-term profit, and if each had full information about the other. Finally, empirical analysis based on a differential game model can yield information about a competitor, such as unit margins, that the manager may not know otherwise.

Whether for academic research or managerial understanding, a differential game interpretation of advertising competition offers the potential for powerful insights. By allowing an expanded notion of what defines advertising strategies, empirical analysis can supplement theoretical development to provide significant advances to our understanding of competitive advertising in dynamic markets.

References

Aaker, David A. and James M. Carman (1982), "Are You Overadvertising?" *Journal of Advertising Research*, 22 (August–September), 57–70.

Assmus, Gert, John U. Farley, and Donald R. Lehmann (1984), "How Advertising Affects Sales: Meta-analysis of Econometric Results," *Journal of Marketing Research*, 21 (February), 65–74.

Bass, Frank M. (1969a), "A Simultaneous Equation Regression Study of Advertising and the Sales of Cigarettes," *Journal of Marketing Research*, 6 (August), 291–300.

Bass, Frank M. (1969b), "New Product Growth Model for Consumer Durables," *Management Science*, 15 (January), 215–227.

Bass, Frank M. and Leonard J. Parsons (1969), "Simultaneous-Equation Regression Analysis of Sales and Advertising," *Applied Economics*, 1 (May), 103–124.

Beckwith, Neil E. (1972), "Multivariate Analysis of Sales Responses of Competing Brands to Advertising," *Journal of Marketing Research*, 9 (May), 168–176.

Bemmaor, Albert C. (1984), "Testing Alternative Econometric Models on the Existence of Advertising Threshold Effect," *Journal of Marketing Research*, 21 (August), 298–308.

Bensoussan, Alain, Alain Bultez, and Philippe Naert (1978), "Leader's Dynamic Marketing Behavior in Oligopoly," *TIMS Studies In the Management Sciences*, 9 Amsterdam: North-Holland, 123–145.

Brown, Randall S. (1978), "Estimating Advantages to Large-scale Advertising," *Review of Economics and Statistics*, 60, 428–437.

Business Week (1982), "Anheuser-Busch: The King of Beers Still Rules," July 12, 50–54.

Business Week (1989), "Coors May Take a Gulp of a Rival Brew," August 21, 70.

Carpenter, Gregory S., Lee G. Cooper, Dominique M. Hanssens, and David F. Midgley (1988), "Modeling Asymmetric Competition," *Marketing Science*, 7 (Fall), 393–412.

Case, James H. (1975), "A Game of Advertising Strategy," *Proceedings of the IFAC 6th World Congress*, Boston/Cambridge MA, part 1, 16.3.1–16.3.3.

Case, James H. (1979), *Economics and the Competitive Process*, New York: New York University Press.

Chatterjee, Rabikar and Jehoshua Eliashberg (1990), "The Innovation Diffusion Process in a Heterogeneous Population: A Micromodeling Approach," *Man-*

agement Science, 36 (September), 1057–1079.

Chintagunta, Pradeep and Naufel J. Vilcassim (1989), "Optimal Resource Allocation in a Dynamic Duopoly," working paper, J. L. Kellogg Graduate School of Management, Northwestern University.

Clarke, Darral G. (1973), "Sales-Advertising Cross-Elasticities and Advertising Competition," *Journal of Marketing Research*, 10 (August), 250–261.

Clarke, Darral G. (1976), "Econometric Measurement of the Duration of Advertising Effect on Sales," *Journal of Marketing Research*, 13 (November), 345–357.

Clarke, Darral G. (1978), "Strategic Advertising Planning: Merging Multidimensional Scaling and Econometric Analysis," *Management Science*, 24 (December), 1687–1699.

Clemhout, S. and H. Y. Wan, Jr. (1979), "Interactive Economic Dynamics and Differential Games," *Journal of Optimization Theory and Applications*, 27 (January), 7–30.

Cooper, Lee G. and Masao Nakanishi (1988), *Market Share Analysis*, Boston: Kluwer Academic Publishers.

Cowling, K., J. Cable, M. Kelly, and T. McGuinness (1975), *Advertising and Economic Behaviour*, New York: Holmes & Meier Publishers.

Deal, K. R. (1979), "Optimizing Advertising Expenditures in a Dynamic Duopoly," *Operations Research*, 27 (July–August), 682–692.

Deal, K.R., S.P. Sethi, and G.L. Thompson (1979), "A Bilinear-Quadratic Differential Game in Advertising," in Pan-Tai Liu and Jon G. Sutinen (eds.), *Control Theory in Mathematical Economics*, New York: Marcel Dekker, 91–109.

Dockner, E., G. Feichtinger, and S. Jørgensen (1985), "Tractable Classes of Nonzero-Sum Open-Loop Nash Differential Games: Theory and Examples," *Journal of Optimization Theory and Applications*, 45 (February), 179–197.

Dockner, Engelbert and Steffen Jørgensen (1988), "Optimal Advertising Policies for Diffusion Models of New Product Innovation in Monopolistic Situations," *Management Science*, 34 (January), 119–130.

Dockner, Engelbert and Steffen Jørgensen (1991), "New Product Advertising in Dynamic Oligopolies," *Zeitschrift für Operations Research*, forthcoming.

Eliashberg, Jehoshua and Rabikar Chatterjee (1985), "Analytical Models of Competition with Implications for Marketing: Issues, Findings, and Outlook," *Journal of Marketing Research*, 22 (August), 237–261.

Erickson, Gary M. (1985), "A Model of Advertising Competition," *Journal of Marketing Research*, 22 (August), 297–304.

Feichtinger, Gustav (1983), "The Nash Solution of an Advertising Differential Game: Generalization of a Model by Leitmann and Schmitendorf," *IEEE Transactions on Automatic Control*, AC-28 (November), 1044–1048.

Feichtinger, G. and E. Dockner (1984), "A Note to Jorgensen's Logarithmic Advertising Differential Game," *Zeitschrift für Operations Research*, 28, B 133–B 153.

Feichtinger, Gustav, Richard F. Hartl, and Suresh Sethi (1989), "Dynamic Optimal Control Models in Advertising: Recent Developments," working paper. Institute for Econometrics, Operations Research and Systems Theory, Technical University, Vienna, Austria and Faculty of Management, University of Toronto, Canada.

Fershtman, Chaim (1984), "Goodwill and Market Shares in Oligopoly," *Economica*, 51 (August), 271–281.

Fershtman, Chaim (1987a), "Alternative Approaches to Dynamic Games," in Ralph C. Bryant and Richard Portes (eds.), *Global Macroeconomics: Policy Conflict and Cooperation*, New York: Macmillan, 43–57.

Fershtman, Chaim (1987b), "Identification of Classes of Differential Games for Which the Open Loop is a Degenerate Feedback Nash Equilibrium," *Journal of Optimization Theory and Applications*, 55 (November), 217–231.

Fershtman, Chaim, Vijay Mahajan, and Eitan Muller (1990), "Market Share Pioneering Advantage: A Theoretical Approach," *Management Science*, 36 (August), 900–918.

Friedman, James W. (1983), "Advertising and Oligopolistic Equilibrium," *Bell Journal of Ecoomics*, 14 (Fall), 464–473.

Friedman, Lawrence (1958), "Game-Theory Models in the Allocation of Advertising Expenditures," *Operations Research*, 6 (September–October), 699–709.

Grabowski, Henry G. and Dennis C. Mueller (1971), "Imitative Advertising in the Cigarette Industry," *Antitrust Bulletin*, 16, 257–292.

Gupta, Shiv K. and K.S. Krishnan (1967), "Mathematical Models in Marketing," *Operations Research*, 15 (November–December), 1040–1050.

Hahn, Minhi and Jin-Sok Hyun (1990), "Advertising Cost Interactions and the Optimality of Pulsing," *Management Science*, forthcoming.

Hanssens, Dominique M. (1980), "Market Response, Competitive Behavior, and Time Series Analysis," *Journal of Marketing Research*, 17 (November), 470–485.

Hanssens, Dominique M., Leonard J. Parsons, and Randall L. Schultz (1990), *Market Response Models: Econometric and Time Series Analysis*, Boston: Kluwer Academic Publishers.

Horsky, Dan (1977), "An Empirical Analysis of the Optimal Advertising Policy," *Management Science*, 23 (June), 1037–1049.

Horsky, Dan and Karl Mate (1988), "Dynamic Advertising Strategies of Competing Durable Good Producers," *Marketing Science*, 7 (Fall), 356–367.

Horsky, Dan and Leonard S. Simon (1983), "Advertising and the Diffusion of New Products," *Marketing Science*, 2 (Winter), 1–17.

Houston, Franklin S. and Doyle L. Weiss (1974), "An Analysis of Competitive Market Behavior," *Journal of Marketing Research*, 11 (May), 151–155.

Jones, Philip C. (1983), "Analysis of a Dynamic Duopoly Model of Advertising," *Mathematics of Operations Research*, 8 (February), 122–134.

Jørgensen, Steffen (1982a), "A Survey of Some Differential Games in Advertising," *Journal of Economic Dynamics and Control*, 4 (November), 341–369.

Jørgensen, Steffen (1982b), "A Differential Games Solution to a Logarithmic Advertising Model," *Journal of the Operational Research Society*, 33 (May), 425–432.

Kamien, Morton I. and Nancy L. Schwartz (1981), *Dynamic Optimization: The Calculus of Variations and Optimal Control in Economics and Management*, New York: North-Holland.

Kelton, Christine M.L. and W. David Kelton (1982), "Advertising and Intra-industry Brand Shift in the U.S. Brewing Industry," *Journal of Industrial Economics*, 30 (March), 292–303.

Kimball, George E. (1957), "Some Industrial Applications of Military Operations Research Methods," *Operations Research*, 5 (April), 201–204.

Kotler, Philip (1988), *Marketing Management: Analysis, Planning, and Control* (sixth edition), Englewood Cliffs, NJ: Prentice-Hall.

Kuehn, Alfred A., Timothy W. McGuire, and Doyle L. Weiss (1966), "Measuring the Effectiveness of Advertising," *Proceedings*, Fall Conference, Chicago: American Marketing Conference, 185–194.

Lambin, Jean-Jacques (1970a), "Optimal Allocation of Competitive Marketing Efforts: An Empirical Study," *Journal of Business*, 43 (October), 468–484.

Lambin, Jean-Jacques (1970b), "Advertising and Competitive Behavior: A Case Study," *Applied Economics*, 2 (January), 231–251.

Lambin, Jean-Jacques (1972), "Is Gasoline Advertising Justified?" *Journal of Business*, 45 (October), 585–619.

Lambin, Jean-Jacques (1976), *Advertising, Competition and Market Conduct in Oligopoly Over Time*, Amsterdam: North-Holland.

Lambin, Jean-Jacques, Philippe A. Naert, and Alain Bultez (1975), "Optimal Marketing Behavior in Oligopoly," *European Economic Review*, 6 (April), 105–128.

Lancaster, Kent M. (1984), "Brand Advertising Competition and Industry Demand," *Journal of Advertising*, 13 (4), 19–30.

Lancaster, Kent M. and Judith A. Stern (1983), "Computer-Based Advertising Budgeting Practices of Leading U.S. Consumer Advertisers," *Journal of Advertising*, 12 (4), 4–9.

Leitmann, G. and W.E. Schmitendorf (1978), "Profit Maximization Through Advertising: A Nonzero Sum Differential Game Approach," *IEEE Transactions on Automatic Control*, AC-23 (August), 645–650.

Little, John D.C. (1979), "Aggregate Advertising Models: The State of the Art," *Operations Research*, 27 (July–August), 629–667.

Mahajan, Vijay, Eitan Muller, and Frank M. Bass (1990), "New Product Diffusion Models in Marketing: A Review and Directions for Research," *Journal of Marketing*, 54 (January), 1–26.

McGuire, Timothy W., John U. Farley, Robert E. Lucas, Jr., and L. Winston Ring (1968), "Estimation and Inference for Linear Models in Which Subsets of the Dependent Variable are Constrained," *Journal of the American Statistical Association*, 63 (December), 1201–1213.

Metwally, M.M. (1975), "Advertising and Competitive Behaviour of Selected Australian Firms," *Review of Economics and Statistics*, 57 (November), 417–427.

Metwally, M.M. (1978), "Escalation Tendencies of Advertising," *Oxford Bulletin of Economics and Statistics*, 40 (May), 153–163.

Mills, Harland D. (1961), "A Study in Promotional Competition," in Frank M. Bass et al. (eds.), *Mathematical Models and Methods in Marketing*, Homewood, IL: Richard D. Irwin, 271–301.

Moorthy, K. Sridhar (1985), "Using Game Theory to Model Competition," *Journal of Marketing Research*, 22 (August), 262–282.

Morris, Betsy (1987), "Coke Vs. Pepsi: Cola War Marches On," *Wall Street Journal*, June 3, 33.

Mukundan, Rangaswamy and Wolfgang B. Elsner (1975), "Linear Feedback Strategies in Non-Zero-Sum Differential Games," *International Journal of Systems Science*, 6 (June), 513–532.

Nakanishi, Masao and Lee G. Cooper (1974), "Parameter Estimation for a Multiplicative Competitive Interaction Model—Least Squares Approach," *Journal of Marketing Research*, 11 (August), 303–311.

Nakashini, Masao and Lee G. Cooper (1982), "Simplified Estimation Procedures for MCI Models," *Marketing Science*, 1 (Summer), 314–322.

Nerlove, Marc and Kenneth J. Arrow (1962), "Optimal Advertising Policy Under Dynamic Conditions," *Economica*, 39 (May), 129–142.

Nguyen, Dung (1987), "Advertising, Random Sales Response, and Brand Competition: Some Thoeretical and Econometric Implications," *Journal of Business*, 60 (April), 259–279.

Olsder, Geert Jan (1976), "Some Thoughts About Simple Advertising Models as Differential Games and the Structure of Coalitions," in Y.C. Ho and S.K. Mitter (eds.), *Directions in Large-Scale Systems, Many-Person Optimization and Decentralized Control*, New York: Plenum Press, 187–205.

Peles, Yoram (1971a), "Economies of Scale in Advertising Beer and Cigarettes," *Journal of Business*, 44 (January), 32–37.

Peles, Yoram (1971b), "Rates of Amortization of Advertising Expenditures," *Journal of Political Economy*, 79 (September–October), 1032–1058.

Picconi, Mario J. and Charles L. Olson (1978), "Advertising Decision Rules in a Multibrand Environment: Optimal Control Theory and Evidence," *Journal of Marketing Research*, 15 (February), 82–92.

Prasad, V. Kanti and L. Winston Ring (1976), "Measuring Sales Effects of Some Marketing Mix Variables and Their Interactions," *Journal of Marketing Research*, 13 (November), 391–396.

Rao, Ram C. (1984), "Advertising Decisions in Oligopoly: An Industry Equilibrium Analysis," *Optimal Control Applications & Methods*, 5 (October–December), 331–344.

Roberts, Mark J. and Larry Samuelson (1988), "An Empirical Analysis of Dynamic, Nonprice Competition in an Oligopolistic Industry," *RAND Journal of Economics*, 19 (Summer), 200–220.

Samuels, J.M. (1971), "The Effect of Advertising on Sales and Brand Shares," *British Journal of Marketing*, 4 (Winter), 187–207.

Schmalensee, Richard (1972), *The Economics of Advertising*, Amsterdam: North-Holland.

Schmalensee, Richard (1976), "A Model of Promotional Competition in Oligopoly," *Review of Economic Studies*, 43 (October), 493–507.

Schmalensee, Richard (1978), "A Model of Advertising and Product Quality," *Journal of Political Economy*, 86 (June), 485–503.

Schnabel, Morton (1972), "An Oligopoly Model of the Cigarette Industry," *Southern Economic Journal*, 38 (January), 325–335.

Schultz, Randall L. (1971), "Market Measurement and Planning With a Simultaneous-Equation Model," *Journal of Marketing Research*, 8 (May), 153–164.

Sethi, Suresh P. (1977), "Dynamic Optimal Control Models in Advertising: A Survey," *SIAM Review*, 19 (October), 685–725.

Sexton, Donald E., Jr. (1970), "Estimating Marketing Policy Effects on Sales of a Frequently Purchased Product," *Journal of Marketing Research*, 7 (August), 338–347.

Shakun, Melvin F. (1965), "Advertising Expenditures in Coupled Markets—A Game-Theory Approach," *Management Science*, 11 (February), B42–B47.

Shakun, Melvin F. (1966), "A Dynamic Model for Competitive Marketing in Coupled Markets," *Management Science*, 12 (August), B525–B529.

Simon, Hermann and Karl-Heinz Sebastian (1987), "Diffusion and Advertising: The German Telephone Campaign," *Management Science*, 33 (April), 451–466.

Sorger, Gerhard (1989), "Competitive Dynamic Advertising: A Modification of the Case Game," *Journal of Economic Dynamics and Control*, 13 (January), 55–80.

Starr, A.W. and Y.C. Ho (1969), "Nonzero-sum Differential Games," *Journal of Optimization Theory and Applications*, 3 (March), 184–219.

Tang, Y. Edwin (1990), "A Dynamic Model of Market Share Competition and Optimal Advertising," paper presented at Marketing Science Conference, University of Illinois, March 22–25.

Tapiero, Charles S. (1979), "A Generalization of the Nerlove–Arrow Model to Multi-Firms Advertising Under Uncertainty," *Management Science*, 25 (September), 907–915.

Telser, Lester G. (1962), "Advertising and Cigarettes," *Journal of Political Economy*, 70 (October), 471–499.

Teng, Jinn-Tsair and Gerald L. Thompson (1983), 'Oligopoly Models for Optimal Advertising When Production Costs Obey a Learning Curve," *Management Science*, 29 (September), 1087–1101.

Thépot, Jacques (1983), "Marketing and Investment Policies of Duopolists in a Growing Industry," *Journal of Economic Dynamics and Control*, 5 (July), 387–404.

Thompson, Gerald L. and Jinn-Tsair Teng (1984), "Optimal Pricing and Advertising Policies for New Product Oligopoly Models," *Marketing Science*, 3 (Spring), 148–168.

Vidale, M.L. and H.B. Wolfe (1957), "An Operations Research Study of Sales Response to Advertising," *Operations Research*, 5 (June), 370–381.

Weiss, Doyle L. (1968), "Determinants of Market Share," *Journal of Marketing Research*, 5 (August), 290–295.

Weiss, Doyle L. (1969), "An Analysis of the Demand Structure for Branded Consumer Products," *Applied Economics*, 1 (January), 37–49.

Wildt, Albert R. (1974), "Multifirm Analysis of Competitive Decision Variables," *Journal of Marketing Research*, 11 (November), 50–62.

Wittink, Dick R. (1977), "Exploring Territorial Differences in the Relationship Between Marketing Variables," *Journal of Marketing Research*, 14 (May), 145–155.

Wrather, C. and P.L. Yu (1979), "Advertising Games in Duopoly Market Expansion," in Pan-Tai Liu and Jon G. Sutinen (eds.), *Control Theory in Mathematical Economics*, New York: Marcel Dekker, 111–149.

Zufryden, Fred S. (1975), "Optimal Multi-Period Advertising Budget Allocation Within a Competitive Environment," *Operational Research Quarterly*, 26 (June), 743–754.

Author Index

119

120

Subject Index

121